mu

BAH

Snorkeling in the Abacos ©The Bahamas Ministry of Tourism

Editorial Director	Cynthia Clayton Ochterbeck

mustsees Bahamas

Editor	Rachel Mills
Writer	Jessica Robertson
Contributing Writer	Sara Macefield
Production Manager	Natasha G. George
Cartography	Peter Wrenn
Photo Editor	Yoshimi Kanazawa
Photo Research	Claudia Tate
Layout	John Higginbottom, Natasha G. George
Cover & Interior Design	Chris Bell

Contact Us:

Michelin Maps and Guides
One Parkway South
Greenville, SC 29615
USA
www.michelintravel.com
michelin.guides@us.michelin.com

Michelin Maps and Guides
Hannay House
39 Clarendon Road
Watford, Herts WD17 1JA
UK
☎(01923) 205 240
www.ViaMichelin.com
travelpubsales@uk.michelin.com

Special Sales:

For information regarding bulk sales, customized
editions and premium sales, please contact
our Customer Service Departments:

USA	1-800-432-6277
UK	(01923) 205 240
Canada	1-800-361-8236

Michelin Apa Publications Ltd

A joint venture between Michelin and Langenscheidt

58 Borough High Street, London SE1 1XF, United Kingdom

No part of this publication may be reproduced in any form
without the prior permission of the publisher.

© 2009 Michelin Apa Publications Ltd
ISBN 978-1-906261-62-7
Printed: December 2008
Printed and bound: Himmer, Germany

Note to the reader:

Welcome to the Bahamas

Beach on Cat Island

© Bahamas Tourist Office

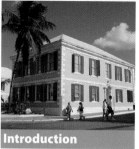

Introduction

Bahamas: History   **26**

Must See

New Providence:
Nassau   **30**
A Providential Place   30
Nassau Proper   31
  Resorts and Spas   **32**
  Casinos   **37**
  Beaches   **38**
  Historic Buildings   **39**
  Museums and Galleries   **43**
  Parks and Gardens   **45**
  Historic Sites   **46**
  Must Do   **48**
  Walking Tour   48
  Driving Tour   50
  For Kids   52
  Shopping   54
  Outdoor Sports   56
  Watersports   58
  Nightlife   62

Paradise Island   **64**
Hog Island to Paradise   64
  Resorts and Spas   **65**
  Casinos   **69**
  Beaches   **70**
  Historic Buildings   **71**
  Must Do   **72**
  Shopping   72

Outdoor Sports   73
Watersports   74
Nightlife   76

Grand Bahama Island:
Freeport & Lucaya   **78**
Freeport   79
Lucaya   79
  Resorts   **80**
  Casinos   **83**
  Beaches   **84**
  Parks and Gardens   **86**
  Natural Sites   **88**
  Historic Sites   **89**
  Must Do   **90**
  Shopping   90
  Nature Tours   92
  Outdoor Sports   93
  Watersports   94
  Nightlife   98

Andros, Berry and
Bimini Islands   **100**
Andros   100
The Berry Islands   101
The Bimini Islands   101
  Resorts and Spas   **102**
  Beaches   **107**
  Museums   **108**
  Parks and Gardens   **109**
  Natural Sites   **110**
  Historic Sites   **111**

p 78

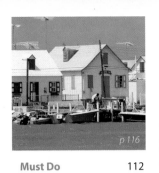

p 116

Must Do	**112**
Watersports	112

Abacos: Great Abacos,
Little Abacos **116**
Great Abaco: Marsh Harbour
  & Treasure Cay 116
Hope Town, Man O'War, Green
  Turtle & Great Guana Cay 116
Resorts 117
Historic Buildings 121
Museums and Galleries 123
Parks and Gardens 124

Must Do **126**
Watersports 126

Eleuthera, Harbour
Island & Spanish Wells 128
Eleuthera 128
Harbour Island &
  Spanish Wells 128
Resorts 129
Beaches 132
Natural Sites 134

Must Do **136**
Watersports 136
Nightlife 137

The Exumas:
Great Exuma, Little
Exuma, Exuma Cays **138**
Great Exuma & Little Exuma 138
The Exuma Cays 138

Resorts 139
Beaches 140
Natural Sites 142

Must Do **144**
Outdoor Sports 144
Watersports 144

South Islands **146**
Acklins Island 146
Cat Island 146
Crooked island 146
Inagua 146
Long Island 147
San Salvador 147
Resorts 148
Beaches 152
Historic Buildings
  and Museums 154
Parks and Gardens 156
Natural Sites 157
Historic Sites 158

Must Do **159**
Watersports 159
Nightlife 161

Must Eat
Restaurants 162

Must Stay
Hotels 174

Must Know
Star Attractions 6
Calendar of Events 12
Practical Information 16
Index 186
Map Index 192

TABLE OF CONTENTS

★★★ ATTRACTIONS

Unmissable attractions awarded stars in this guide include:

© The Bahamas Ministry of Tourism

Dean's Blue Hole, Long Island   p 157, 159

© Powerboat Adventures/Bahamas Tourist Office

Andros Barrier Reef, Andros   p 112

Exuma Cays p 138

©Ray Wadia/The Bahamas Ministry of Tourism

Pink Sands Beach, Harbour Island p 132

© Bahamas Tourist Office

Christ Church Cathedral, Nassau p 39

© The Bahamas Ministry of Tourism

Hope Town Lighthouse, the Abacos p 121

©Bahamas Tourist Office

Lucayan National Park, Grand Bahama p 86

© The Bahamas Ministry of Tourism

STAR ATTRACTIONS

ACTIVITIES

The Michelin Man's top tips in this guide include:

© The Bahamas Ministry of Tourism

Shark Dives in Nassau p 59

© Bahamas Tourist Office

Shopping at Port Lucaya, Grand Bahama p 90

© Derek Smith/The Bahamas Ministry of Tourism

Columbus Landing Cross, San Salvador p 158

© The Bahamas Ministry of Tourism

Renting a boat in the Abacos   p 126

© Progressive Earth Development/ Bahamas Tourist Office

Eco-friendly Tiamo Resorts, Andros   p 104

© 2005 Lars Topelmann/The Bahamas Ministry of Tourism

Iguanas at Allan's Cay, Exuma Cays   p 142

©Peter Vitale/Atlantis

Atlantis Casino, Paradise Island   p 69

©Bahamas Tourist Office

Rock House, Harbour Island   p 130

★★★ ATTRACTIONS

Unmissable sights in the Bahamas

For more than 75 years people have used the Michelin stars to take the guesswork out of travel. Our star-rating system helps you make the best decision on where to go, what to do, and what to see.

★★★	Absolutely Must See
★★	Really Must See
★	Must See
No Star	See

★★★ Three-Star Sights

Andros Barrier Reef *p 112*

★★ Two-Star Sights

Nassau (New Providence) *p 30*
Lucayan National Park
(Grand Bahama) *p 86*
Pink Sands Beach
(Harbour Island) *p 132*
The Exuma Cays *p 138*
Exuma Cay Land and Sea Park *p 142*
Thunderball Grotto
(The Exumas) *p 144*
Cape Santa Maria Beach
(Long Island) *p 152*
Dean's Blue Hole
(Long Island) *p 157, 159*
Inagua National Park *p 156*

★ One-Star Sights

Cable Beach
(New Providence) *p 38*
Pleasant Bay
(New Providence) *p 38*
Christ Church Cathedral
(New Providence) *p 39*
Fort Charlotte
(New Providence) *p 39*

National Art Gallery of the
Bahamas (New Providence) *p 43*
Straw Market
(New Providence) *p 55*
Palms at the Retreat Gardens
(New Providence) *p 46*
Views from the Water Tower
(New Providence) *p 46*
Cabbage Beach
(Paradise Island) *p 70*
Fortune Beach
(Grand Bahama) *p 84*
Rand Nature Center
(Grand Bahama) *p 86*
Taino Beach (Grand Bahama) *p 84*
Summer Set Beach (Andros) *p 107*
Albert Lowe Museum
(Abacos) *p 123*
Hope Town Lighthouse
(Abacos) *p 121*
Dunmore Town
(Harbour Island) *p 128*
The Glass Window
(Eleuthera) *p 134*
Ocean Hole (Eleuthera) *p 134*
Mount Alvernia Hermitage
(Cat Island) *p 154*
Views from Dixon Hill Lighthouse
(San Salvador) *p 154*

MUST KNOW

ACTIVITIES

Unmissable Bahamas tours, festivals, snorkel sites and more
The Bahamas offer a tropical climate, pristine beaches, turquoise waters and numerous activities to make the most of your vacation. We recommend every activity in this guide, but the Michelin Man highlights our top picks.

Diving & Snorkeling
Dive with Sharks
(New Providence) *p 59*
Snorkel Peterson's Cay National Park (Grand Bahama) *p 97*
Dive or Snorkel Andros Barrier Reef *p 112*
Drift Diving at Current Cut (Eleuthera) *p 136*

Entertainment
Junkanoo (New Providence) *p 31*
Junkanoo at Marina Village (Paradise Island) *p 77*
Atlantis Casino (Paradise Island) *p 69*
Gusty's Bar (Harbour Island) *p 137*
Club Med (San Salvador) *p 161*

On the Water
Bonefishing in Andros *p 114*
Big Game Fishing in Bimini *p 114*
Renting a boat in the Abacos *p 126*

Shopping
Port Lucaya (Grand Bahama) *p 90*

Top Eateries
Arawak Cay (New Providence) *p 47*
Bobby Flay's Mesa Grill (The Cove, Atlantis, Paradise Island) *p 165*
Wednesday Night at Smith's Point Fish Fry (Grand Bahama) *p 89*
Kamalame Cay Resort Restaurant (Andros) *p 168*
Long lunch at Sip Sip (Harbour Island) *p 171*

Pig Roast at Stocking Island (The Exumas) *p 141*

Top Resorts
Marley Resort and Spa (New Providence) *p 32, 175*
Sivananda Yoga Retreat *p 67, 179*
Eco-friendly Tiamo Resorts (Andros) *p 104*
Rock House Resort (Harbour Island) *p 130, 184*
Cape Santa Maria Beach Resort (Long Island) *p 148, 185*

Culture
Johnston's Foundry and Gallery (Abacos) *p 123*
Columbus Landing Cross (San Salvador) *p 158*

Nature
Dolphin Encounters (New Providence) *p 52*
Segway Bahamas (New Providence) *p 57*
Smiling Pat's Adventures (Grand Bahama) *p 88*
Bird Watching in Abaco National Park *p 124*
Iguanas at Allan's Cay (The Exumas) *p 142*

Remember to look out for the Michelin Man for top activities.

STAR ATTRACTIONS

CALENDAR OF EVENTS

Listed below are some of the The Bahamas' most popular events.
Please note that specific dates may vary from year to year.
For more detailed information contact the Bahamas Tourist Office
(242-302-2000; www.bahamas.com/bahamas.co.uk).

January
New Year Junkanoo Parade
Annual Carnival celebration
    Bay Street, Nassau
    242-356-2691
    www.junkanoo.com
Near Year's Day
Junkanoo Parade
Annual Carnival celebration
    New Plymouth, The Abacos
    242-367-3067
    www.bahamas.com

February
People-to-People/Winter
Residents' Reception
Get-together with local residents
    Treasure Cay, The Abacos
    242-367-3067
    www.bahamas.com

March
Cricket season begins
Matches every weekend from
March to November

    Haynes Oval, Nassau
    242-326-4720
    www.bahamas.com

April
Authentically Grand
Bahamian Crafts and Fine Art
Local handicrafts fair
    Freeport and Taino Beach,
    Grand Bahama Island
    242-302-2000
    www.bahamas.co.uk
Abaco Anglers Fishing
Tournament
Family-orientated deep sea and
bottom fishing tournament
    Elbow Cay, The Abacos
    242-366-0154
    www.bahamas.co.uk
Bahamas White Marlin Open
Three-day fishing tournament
    Treasure Cay Beach Resort,
    The Abacos
    242-365-8801
    www.treasurecay.com

January & July: Junkanoo, Nassau

© The Bahamas Ministry of Tourism

MUST KNOW

International Legends of Diving
Diving summit
  Grand Bahama Island
  242-373-1244
  www.bahamas.com

May

Bertram Hatteras Shootout (Billfish Tourney)
One of the best fishing tournaments in the Abacos
  The Abacos
  242-367-2158
  www.bahamas.co.uk

Sea Spray Resort Fishing Tournament
Contest to catch Blue Marlin and Tuna
  Elbow Cay, The Abacos
  242-366-0065
  www.seasprayresort.com

June

Bahamas Rotary Tuna Classic Annual Tournament
Deep sea fishing contest
  Paradise Island
  242-394-9980
  www.bahamas.co.uk

Annual Grand Bahama Island Sailing Regatta
Sloop races and beach parties
  Taino Beach, Grand Bahama Island
  242-352-8044
  www.bahamas.co.uk

Annual Treasure Cay Billfish Championship
One of the main Abaco fishing events
  Treasure Cay Beach Resort, The Abacos
  242-365-8801
  www.treasurecay.com

Bahamas Billfish Boat Harbour Championship
Premier event with big

prize-money
  The Abacos
  242-367-2158
  www.abacobeachresort.co.uk

Junkanoo Summer Festival
Carnival celebrations
  Marsh Harbour, The Abacos
  242-367-3067
  www.bahamas.co.uk

Junkanoo Summer Festival
Carnival celebrations
  The Exumas
  242-336-2430
  www.bahamas.co.uk

July: Regatta, the Abacos

© The Bahamas Ministry of Tourism

July

Independence Day
Junkanoo Rush-Out
Carnival celebrations
  East Bay Street, Nassau
  242-356-2691
  www.bahamas.co.uk

Junkanoo Summer Festival
Carnival celebrations
  Nassau
  242-302-2000
  www.jsf.bahamas.co.uk

Annual Five Towns Regatta Time
Sailing competition linked to US and Bahamian independence celebrations
  The Abacos
  242-367-2343
  www.bahamas.co.uk

August: Regatta, the Exumas

©The Bahamas Ministry of Tourism

**North Abaco Summer Festival
& Powerboat Race**
Racing and cultural event
 The Abacos
 242-475-3275
 www.bahamas.com
Barefoot Man Concert
Live entertainment
 Nippers Beach Bar & Grill,
 Guana Cay, The Abacos
 242-365-5143
 www.nippersbar.com

August
Lobster Fest
Lobster cooked anyway you
want it
 Bimini
 242-347-3529
 www.bahamas.co.uk
**Emancipation Day
Rolleville Regatta**
A weekend of racing and festivities
 The Exumas
 242-345-6002
 www.bahamas.co.uk

September
**College of the Bahamas
Jazz Under the Stars Festival**
Live jazz and gourmet dining
 Nassau
 242-302-4304
 www.bahamas.co.uk

October
**Bahamas National Trust
Annual Wine & Art Festival**
Showcases local art and produce
 The Retreat, Village Road,
 Nassau
 242-393-1317
 www.bahamas. com
**Grand Bahama Discovery
Street Festival**
Cultural performances
 Grand Bahama Island
 242-352-8044
 www.bahamas.co.uk
**Pirates of Grand
Bahama Dive Week**
Diving and entertainment
 Grand Bahama Island
 242-350-8600
 www.bahamas.com
**Chickcharnie Festival &
North Andros Seafood Splash**
Cultural and culinary fiesta
 Andros
 242-368-2286
 www.bahamas.com

November
Christmas Jollification
Arts & crafts festival
 The Retreat, Village Road,
 Nassau
 242-393-1317
 www.bahamas.co.uk

Annual Brietling
Golf Tournment
One of the major golfing events
    The Reef and Lucayan golf
    courses, Grand Bahama Island
    242-352-7835
    www.bahamas.co.uk
Annual Guy Fawkes Festival
Fireworks celebration
    Williams Town, Grand Bahama
    Island
    242-352-8044
    www.bahamas.co.uk
Annual Grand Bahama
Conchman Triathlon
For sporting enthusiasts
    Taino Beach, Grand Bahama
    Island
    242-373-6226
    www.conchman.com
Hope Town Big Hill
Box Cart Derby
Cart races
    Hope Town, Abaco
    242-366-3139
    www.bahamas.com

December
Junior Junkanoo Parade
Children's carnival celebration
    Downtown Nassau
    242-356-2691
    www.junkanoo.com

Junkanoo Boxing Day Parade
Carnival celebration
    Bay Street, Nassau
    242-302-2000
    www.junkanoo.co.uk
Renaissance Singers
Christmas Concert
Classical, modern and ethnic
Christmas music
    Government House, Nassau
    242-302-4512/328 8553
    www.bahamas.co.uk
Bahamas International
Film Festival
Showcasing Bahamian films
    Nassau
    242-356-5939
    www.bintlfilmfest.com
Junkanoo—Eleuthera
Carnival celebrations
    Tarpum Bay, Rock Sound and
    Harbour Island
    242-332-2142
    www.bahamas.co.uk
Holmes Rock Gospel
Celebration & Cultural Fest
Gospel music and heritage event
    Holmes Rock Park, Grand
    Bahama Island
    242-350-8606
    www.bahamas.com

December: Junior Junkanoo Parade, Nassau

15

PRACTICAL INFORMATION

WHEN TO GO

The Bahamas enjoys a warm temperate climate that hardly varies throughout the year, thanks to the archipelago's gentle trade winds. The months between September and May are fresher with temperatures averaging between 70–75 degrees Farenheit (21–24 degrees Celsius), while the summer tends to be warmer and more humid with temperatures between 80–85 degrees Farenheit (21–24 degrees Celsius). On the more northerly islands winter temperatures are around five degrees lower than on the southern islands while at night, temperatures are around five to seven degrees cooler across all the islands. It can rain at any time during the year, though the official rainy season is May to October. The northern islands generally experience twice as much rain as the southern islands with heavy storms or squalls which quickly clear. From June to November is hurricane season when the islands can be affected by tropical storms and high winds.

KNOW BEFORE YOU GO

It always helps to plan your trip in advance to get the best out of the Bahamas. With so many islands to choose from and so much to do, a little pre-planning goes a long way.

Useful Websites

Take your pick from the websites run by the Bahamas Ministry of Tourism or the numerous tourist-orientated websites that highlight the islands' main attractions.

www.bahamas.com—This is the official site of the Bahamas Ministry of Tourism and it contains comprehensive information about the islands and activities available.
www.bahamas.co.uk—The Bahamas Ministry of Tourism website which is aimed at the UK market. It contains similar details to the bahamas.com site.
www.myoutislands.com—This is the official website for the Bahama Out Islands Promotion Board which gives details of the most popular Out Islands. This includes information on hotels, activities and the best means of getting to each island.
www.nassauparadiseisland.com—This site represents the Nassau/Paradise Island Promotion board, giving details of the hotels and attractions in Nassau and Paradise Island, plus the latest special offers.
www.grandbahamavacations.com—This is the website of the Grand Bahama Island Tourism Board, giving details of what to do and where to stay on the island.

Tourist Offices

The headquarters of the Bahamas Ministry of Tourism is in the capital Nassau. It's address is:
PO Box N-3701
Tel: 242-502-9150/1
Toll free: 1-800-Bahamas

On the other islands the details are as follows:
Grand Bahama Island, Freeport/Lucaya Office,
PO Box F-40251
Tel: 242-352-8044

Average Seasonal Temperatures in the Bahamas				
	Jan	Apr	July	Oct
Avg. High	77°F/25°C	82°F/28°C	88°F/31°C	85°F/29°C
Avg. Low	61°F/16°C	68°F/20°C	75°F/24°C	72°F/22°C

Eleuthera
Sunset House, Queen's Highway,
Governor's Harbour.
Tel: 242-332-2142

Dunmore Street, Harbour Island,
Tel: 242-333-2621

Abaco
Memorial Plaza, Suite #103,
Marsh Harbour.
Tel: 242-367-3067

Exuma
PO Box EX-29041, George Town.
Tel: 242-336-2430/2456/7/8

Andros
Queen's Highway & Lighthouse
Drive,
Central Andros/Fresh Creek.
Tel: 242-368-2286

Mangrove Cay/Victoria Point
Tel: 242-369-0544

South Andros/Congo Town
242-369-1688

Long Island
PO Box 30055, Deals
North Long Island
Tel: 242-338-8668

Bimini
Alice Town
Tel: 242-347-3529

Cat Island
Arthur's Town
Tel: 242-342-3031/2

Visitor Information Booths
There are two at Nassau International Airport, one in arrivals and
one in departures.
Tel: 242-327-6806/6782

There is a booth in Rawson Square,
Bay Street, Nassau
Tel: 242-326-9772/9781

There are also booths in the main
lobby of Festival Place in Nassau
and at Freeport International
Airport and Freeport Harbour
cruise port.

International Visitors

Entry Requirements – Travelers
from the UK do not require a visa
for stays of up to eight months,
just a valid passport that is valid
for at least six months on the date
of departure, proof of funds and
a valid onward or return ticket.
All visitors are required to fill out
and sign an immigration form on
arrival and they keep a portion of
this until they depart. US visitors
need to show a passport, passport
card or Western Hemisphere Travel

Drug Laws
Some travelers have reported
being offered marijuana, particularly in Nassau. Be aware that
the possession of illegal drugs in
the Bahamas is a serious criminal
offence and carries high penalties
such as fines or imprisonment.

Initiative-compliant document such as a driver's licence, and proof of citizenship, such as a birth certificate.

Customs Regulations – Visitors are allowed to bring 50 cigars, 200 cigarettes or one pound of tobacco and a quart of spirits. Various personal possessions, including radio headsets, a bicycle and cameras are also allowed.

Health – No inoculations are necessary unless visitors are traveling from an infected area. The main islands of Nassau/Paradise Island and Grand Bahama Island have good medical facilities staffed by North American and European trained staff.

GETTING THERE

It's easy to get to the Bahamas, which is one reason why the islands are so popular. They can be reached by air or sea, whether it's a short hop by jet, a day-long trip by cruise-ferry, or on a private or charter boat.

By Air

There are nearly 60 airports scattered through the Bahamas, including three international airports and 24 which are designated as official ports of entry to the Bahamas.

The main two airports are:
Nassau International Airport in Nassau *(242-377 1759)*
Freeport International Airport in Freeport, Grand Bahama Island *(242-352 6020)*.
Around 20 airlines fly from the US to the Bahamas, ranging from major carriers such as American Airlines, Continental, Delta, United, Gulfstream and USAirways to regional airlines such as Bahamasair and American Eagle. Local airlines such as Bimini Island Air, Island Express and Lynx Air offer flights from Florida.
Most flights to the Bahamas are from Florida cities such as Miami, Fort Lauderdale, Orlando, Tampa and West Palm Beach. Further afield, they are from New York, Atlanta, Baltimore, Dallas, Chicago, Boston, Washington, Philadelphia, Charlotte and Cincinnati. Most flights are to Nassau, followed by Grand Bahama Island. The main Out Islands served include Exuma, Abaco, Bimini, Andros, Eleuthera.

Airport Transfers – There are no designated transfer services. Taxis are the only form of public transport that serve the airports. Some hotel's organize their own pick-up and drop-off service for guests.

Car Rental		
Car Rental Company	**Reservations**	**Internet**
Avis	242-326-6380	www.avis.com
Budget	242-377-9000	www.budget.com
Dollar	242-325-3716	www.dollar.com
Hertz	242-352-9277	www.hertz.com

By Ship

Discovery Cruise Line offers sailings from Fort Lauderdale to Grand Bahama Island, which take 5hr 15mins. Nassau and Grand Bahama Island are also popular cruise stops for ships sailing southward from Florida toward the Caribbean.

GETTING AROUND

The Bahamas has a good network of flights and ferry services between the islands—which help to transport locals as well as tourists. As most of the services are concentrated on Nassau and Grand Bahama Island, the distances and journey times vary greatly depending on which island you want to visit.

By Road

Taxi – There are numerous taxis and you can flag them down in the street or phone for one. Look out for the Bahamashost sticker in the taxicab window as it means these drivers have been especially trained and approved. You can find taxi stands at most large hotels and at airports at all the islands. Fares are metered and vary between islands, but they are fixed by law. Surcharges often apply for more than two people and for extra luggage.

Bus – In Nassau and Grand Bahama, visitors can jump on the local minibuses—known as jitneys—which generally run from early morning until around 7pm. Fares vary, but are generally around $1 and the correct money is required. The Nassau/Paradise Island jitneys are 32-seater buses and travel to most parts of the island. They operate from 6.30am until 6pm every day, apart from Sundays when there is a limited service. The basic fare is $1 per person and $2 for outlying areas. On Freeport and Paradise Island there are regular shuttle services around the hotels.

Rental cars – Most major car rental firms have offices on Nassau and Grand Bahama, and there are rental desks at most of the major hotels and at the airports. Rental rates are from about $70 a day and the minimum age to hire a car is 25. On the Out Islands, there are small locally-run rental compa-

Important Phone Numbers	
Emergency (24hrs)	**919 or 911**
Police (non-emergency)	242-322-4444
Medical Services:	
Princess Margaret Hospital, Nassau	242-322-2861
Doctors Hospital, Nassau	242-322-8411
Rand Memorial Hospital, Grand Bahama	242-352-6735
Ambulance, Nassau	242-322-2221
Ambulance, Grand Bahama	242-352-2689

Major hotel and motel chains with locations in the Bahamas include:

Property	Phone/Website	Property	Phone/Website
Sandals Resorts	1-888-SANDALS www.sandals.com	Best Western	1-800-780-7234 www.bestwestern.com
SuperClubs	1-877-467-8737 www.superclubs.org	Riu	1-888 666-8816 www.riu.com
Wyndham	1-877-999- 3223 www.wyndham.com	Westin	1-800-937-8461 www.starwoodhotels.com.com
Sheraton	1-800-325-3535 www.starwoodhotels.com	Four Seasons	1-800-819-5053 www.fourseasons.com
Atlantis	1-888-528-7155 www.atlantis.com	Comfort Suites	1-877-424-6423 www.comfortsuites.com

nies. Some hotels also rent cars to guests. Visitors are advised to arrange car hire before they arrive as there is a limited supply on each island.

Scooters – These are available to rent at the main tourist spots and cost around $25 to $35 a day. Helmets must be worn.

Bicycles – These can be hired at the most popular tourist areas or from the hotels. On the Out Islands, where there are less cars, this is an ideal way to explore.

Golf carts – On smaller Out Islands such as Harbour Island, some of the Abacos and Exuma, these are a useful way of getting around and can be hired by the day or the week. As there is only a limited supply, it is best to book one in advance. Some hotels also provide them.

Road Rules – As a former British colony, the Bahamas has maintained the British tradition of driving on the left.

By Air

Inter-island flights – Bahamas-air is the main airline and offers numerous flights from Nassau and Grand Bahama to Out Islands including Abaco, Eleuthera, Exuma, Long Island, Cat Island, San Salvador and other Out Islands. Travellers can also charter their own aircraft from a number of Nassau-based companies including Airstream, Caribbean Aviation, Four Way Charter, Island Helicopters and Take Flight Air Charters.

By Sea

Ferry Services – Travellers wanting to explore the islands in a more leisurely fashion can take their pick from the various ferry services. Bahamas Fast Ferries operates a high-speed 115ft catamaran which runs twice-daily round trips from Nassau to Harbour Island, calling at nearby Spanish Wells and North Eleuthera. The trip takes two hours. It also sails twice-weekly from Nassau to Governor's Harbour in Eleuthera. It costs $110 adults and

$70 for children. The company also offers services to north, central and south Andros, Abaco and Exuma.

Albury's Ferries operates in the Abaco Islands, with services from the capital, Marsh Harbour, to Man-O-War Cay, Hope Town, Guana Cay and Scotland Cays. There are also small local ferry firms on some of the other Out Islands.

Mailboats – One of the most adventurous ways of sailing around the islands is on the battered old mailboats that ply the routes between Nassau and the Out Islands, delivering essentials such as mail, hardware, goats, pigs and whatever else islanders need. The trips on these diesel-powered vessels take from five to 21 hours and they are definitely not for the faint-hearted. Accommodation is basic and it is worth noting where the life rafts are as a few mailboats have run into trouble during storms. To get from Nassau to North Eleuthera or North Andros takes around five hours and costs $20–$30, while Nassau to Long Island takes 15 hours and costs $45.

On Foot

Exploring the capital Nassau is easy by foot. The central area around Bay Street, which is the main shopping area, is compact and easy to wander around and streets are clearly signposted. On Grand Bahama Island, Freeport is more spread out, though the International Bazaar shopping area is good to explore on foot as is the Port Lucaya Marketplace, four miles away. In the Out Islands, places are more spread out, though Harbour Island, Eleuthera,

lends itself to wandering around with its pretty clapboard houses and tiny streets.

BASIC INFORMATION

Accessibility

Disabled Travelers – There are facilities for less able-bodied travelers. At Nassau's international airport there are ramps, adapted toilets, lifts and dedicated parking spaces. Many of the larger and more modern hotels in the Bahamas have specific facilities for disabled travelers with specially-adapted rooms.

Accommodation

For a list of suggested accommodations, see Must Stay.

Hotel Reservation Services

From North America: Bahamas Gateway, *001-877-827-6451, www.bahamasgateway.com*

From the UK: Bahamas Hotels, *0800-048-3390, www.bahamashotels.co.uk*

From Europe: Hotel Reservations Service, *0870-243-0003, www.hrs.com*

Guest-houses – There are a few guest-houses sprinkled across the islands. These are run by locals and are a good way to add more of a local flavour to your stay. The houses tend to be modest, but they are ideal bases for travelers wanting to explore the locality while enjoying home-cooked food. And guests can always pick up local tips on where to go from the owners.

Fishing Lodges – These can be found on the more far-flung

21

Measurement Equivalents										
Degrees Fahrenheit	95°	86°	77°	68°	59°	50°	41°	32°	23°	14°
Degrees Celsius	35°	30°	25°	20°	15°	10°	5°	0°	-5°	-10°

1 inch = 2.5 centimeters	1 foot = 30.5 centimeters
1 mile = 1.6 kilometers	1 pound = 0.4 kilograms
1 quart = 0.9 liters	1 gallon = 3.8 liters

reaches of Grand Bahama Island and in the Out Islands, particularly on the Abacos, Exumas or Andros. They tend to be in idyllic locations away from developed areas and, in some cases, close to the sand flats where the elusive bonefish are found.

Business Hours

Most shops and other businesses tend to open Monday to Friday. Banks on Nassau and Grand Bahama open Monday to Thursday from 9.30am–3pm and on Fridays from 9.30am–5pm. Post offices open from 9am–5pm Monday to Friday and 9am–12.30pm on Saturdays. Shops open from 9am–6pm Monday to Saturday and some open on Sunday. On the Out Islands, shops are more likely to be closed on Sundays.

Communications

Telecommunications are on a par with those in the USA and Canada. The country's telecoms system is BaTelCo. Direct dial phone links are available on most of the islands and the majority of hotels have internet facilities. Mobile phones also work on the islands, though the system is orientated toward North American networks so may not be accessible for European-based mobiles.

Telephone Codes – the international dialling code for the Bahamas is 242. From the UK it is 00 1 242. To dial out from the Bahamas, the code is 1 800. Hotel rates for long-distance phonecalls can be very expensive. It is much better value to buy phonecards that can be used in Bahamian phone boxes, and can be bought at BaTelCo locations throughout the islands.

Internet – This is available throughout the islands. Most hotels have internet facilities and there are also internet cafes in Nassau, Grand Bahama Island and most Out Islands.

Discount Booking Websites

There is a huge choice of such sites, some of which are linked to established travel companies. Expedia is one of the biggest and this powers the holiday search site on the official Bahamas Ministry of Tourism website at www.bahamas. com. *See the sidebar above, right for more sites.*

Electricity

At 120 volts/60 cycles, it is similar to the US so for British and European appliances a US adaptor is required.

Expedia	1-800-397-3342	www.expedia.com
Travelocity	1-888-872-8356	www.travelocity.com
Hotels.com	1-800-246-8357	www.hotels.com
Booking.com	1-888-850-3958	www.booking.com

Media

The Bahamas has its own newspapers, a TV station and numerous radio stations. Satellite TV, providing a full range of US programs, can be found across all the islands.

Newspapers and Magazines

– The Bahamas has three national newspapers: the Nassau Guardian, The Tribune and the Bahama Journal. On Grand Bahama the Freeport News is published Monday to Friday. The Nassau Guardian also publishes local editions for the other islands including the Freeport News, Andros Chronicles, Exuma Sentinel, Eleuthera Advocate and Long Island Mail.

There are also regular tourist newspapers giving details of local events and attractions. Foreign newspapers such as The Daily Telegraph, The Times, Wall Street Journal and New York Times are also sold at hotels and news stands.

Money

Currency Exchange

– The Bahamas has its own national currency, the Bahamian dollar, which holds the same value as the US dollar. However, US dollars are also freely accepted across the island and both currencies are interchangeable. Credit cards are widely accepted at major tourist hotels and larger stores, though small hotels, guest-houses and local restaurants tend to accept only cash. There are ATMs in Nassau/Paradise Island, Grand Bahama Island, Abaco, Exuma, Eleuthera and Harbour Island. Dollar denomination travellers' cheques are also widely accepted.

Public holidays

New Year's Day—January 1
Junkanoo parades take place in most islands

Good Friday—March or April
Most Bahamians attend church services and serve fish as their main meal

Easter Monday—March or April
Marks the start of the "Beach Picnicking" season for Bahamians.

In the News—Papers, Radio & Television

The Bahamas has two main national newspapers: the Nassau Guardian which dates from 1844 and the Tribune, which is published every day apart from Sunday. Both are based in Nassau, along with the Bahama Journal which is published once a week. There are more than 12 radio stations in the islands, three AM and the rest FM, plus one television station ZNS which is owned by the government. *Nassau Guardian, Carter Street, Oakes Field, PO Box N-3011, Nassau. 242 302 2300. www.thenassauguardian.com.*

Several events are held including "cookouts" in public parks on the Nassau waterfront, homecomings and regattas in some of the Out Islands.

Whit Monday—Seventh Monday after Easter

Labor Day—first Friday in June
This is marked with a large parade through the streets of downtown Nassau made up of members of labour unions and the Bahamas political parties.

It starts around 10am and is led by local bands and junkanooers and ends at the Southern Recreation Grounds when local politicians and union leaders give speeches.

Independence Day—July 10

Emancipation Day/August Monday—first Monday in August
This celebrates the emancipation of slavery in the British Colonies in 1834. It is marked with a Junkanoo Rush-out and with a day of beach activities, sailing and regattas in Nassau (New Providence) and the Out Islands. The former slave villages of Gambier and Fox Hill on Nassau have their own special celebrations.

Getting Married

It is quick and easy to marry in the Bahamas and there are some amazing locations where couples can exchange vows. You can choose to marry barefoot on a beach or have a more traditional ceremony in a church. Or perhaps say your vows in the botanical gardens, on a yacht, while swimming with dolphins, or scuba diving! There is a $100 license fee. For information contact the Registrar General in Nassau. *PO Box N-532, Nassau, 242-323-059-4/5/7.*

Discovery Day or Hero's Day
—October 13
This holiday was known as Discovery or Columbus Day, marking the islands' discovery, but in recent years there has been a campaign to change it to Hero's Day in honour of Bahamian National Heroes. A small ceremony is held in Rawson Square, downtown Nassau, in their honour.

Christmas Day—December 25

Boxing Day—December 26
This is named after the boxes that were given to slaves as leftovers from their master's gifts. The boxes were usually sent from England and were well crafted from fine wood. The day was granted to slaves as a holiday. Now it is marked by Junkanoo parades on some of the islands.

Restaurants

For a list of suggested restaurants, see Must Eat.

Diners in the Bahamas can choose from the whole spectrum of dining choices. The islands boast a wide range of upmarket fine dining at gourmet restaurants, some of which are run by famous chefs such as Bobby Flay or Nobu Matsuhisa. Then there are more locally-run eateries serving up delicious traditional dishes along with local entertainment. Some of the tastiest morsels can be found at the regular fish fry evenings— lively beachside gatherings where the fish is cooked in front of you or at some of the local stalls serving up snacks. It's here in the capital of Nassau and on nearby Paradise Island that visitors will find the greatest choice of places to eat with restaurants offering everything from Mexican and

Creole dishes to Chinese, Indian, or
Japanese cuisine.

Smoking

Smoking in the Bahamas is not
banned, but there are smoking and non-smoking areas in
restaurants.

Spectator Sports

The biggest spectator sport is
baseball. It was introduced to
the islands by sailors from the
American war ships that used
to dock at Nassau. In 1954 the
Bahamas Baseball Association
was formed, marking the start of
organized baseball in the islands.
The first organized series of games
ran that year, continuing until 1987
when the association was restruc-
tured. Now baseball is the most
popular sport in the Bahamas. The
second-most popular spectator
sport is cricket. The season runs
from March to November when
matches are played every Saturday
and Sunday at the Haynes Oval on
West Bay Street in Nassau. There
are two major cricket tournaments
held each year. The first is held during the Easter festival where teams
fly in from destinations including
the UK, USA and Hong Kong;
and the second is held over the
Thanksgiving weekend at the end
of November. On Grand Bahama
Island, matches take place at the
Lucaya Cricket Club on Baloa Road,
a five-minute walk from the Lucaya
Golf and Country Club.

Taxes

Visitors to the Bahamas can enjoy
tax-free shopping, with prices said
to be 25% to 50% lower than they
are in the USA. The best savings
are on perfumes and fragrances,
crystal and leather goods, jewelry,
linens, watches, photographic
equipment and china.

Temperature and Measurement

The Bahamas tend to use the Imperial system of measurements so
distances are in miles and weights
are in pounds and ounces. Temperatures also tend to be recorded
in Farenheit rather than Celsius.

Time

The Bahamas observes Eastern
Standard Time, putting it on the
same time as the US East Coast.
It is –5 hours GMT. From March
to November, the islands adopt
Daylight Saving Time.

Tipping

Gratuities are on a par with those
in the United States, with 15%
regarded as the appropriate
amount. Many restaurants and
other establishments include it in
bills automatically, so it is worth
checking to avoid paying twice.
Bellboys and porters usually
receive $1 per bag.

PRACTICAL INFORMATION

BAHAMAS

This collection of 700 coral islands, strung like a precious necklace across 100,000 miles of shallow seas, makes up a country of contrasts that boasts a rich history of piracy, purists and patriotism combined with stunning scenic beauty, unbeatable sporting challenges and some of the best hotels in the world. The Islands of the Bahamas, sit in the Atlantic Ocean, just off the coast of Florida, and have been blessed with crystal clear waters that have made them one of the world's most idyllic and beautiful destinations.

The Bahamas welcomed their first tourist in the 15th century when legendary explorer **Christopher Columbus** arrived in his quest to find the New World. Noting the perilously shallow waters that surrounded the islands, he gave them their name which comes from the Spanish baja mar, meaning low sea. The waters went on to claim many of the Spanish pioneers' ships, but today they attract millions of visitors who are drawn by their mesmerizing scenic beauty as well as some of the best diving, sailing and fishing in the world.

Most of the 3.5 million visitors who arrive each year, step off the many cruise ships that ply these waters, and tend to just visit the main islands of **New Providence★**—

also called Nassau, after the country's capital—and **Freeport** on **Grand Bahama** Island. But to only visit these islands gives just a partial flavor of what this tropical archipelago offers. The Bahamas is a split personality with two very different faces and this is what makes it so appealing. On the one hand it is brash, extravagant and exciting with a promise of non-stop action: on the other it is quiet, quaint, laid-back and reminiscent of a bygone age.

While the capital **Nassau★★**, and it's tiny neighbor **Paradise Island**, may hog the limelight with their lavish casinos and extravagant hotels; the Bahamas' lesser-known isles, such as the **Abacos**, **Eleuthera**, **Harbour Island** and the

House of Assembly, downtown Nassau

©Ray Wadia/The Bahamas Ministry of Tourism

Locals relaxing under the shade, the Exumas

©Bahamas Tourist Office

Exumas, offer an undiscovered, rustic alternative which many feel represents the real spirit of the country. On these numerous islands and cays—known collectively as the **Out Islands** or sometimes referred to as the **Family Islands** (their previous name)—old traditions still survive, having been handed down over hundreds of years in small communities descended from the early settlers. Columbus may have been the first explorer to set foot in the Bahamas—landing on the island of Guanahani in 1492 which he renamed **San Salvador**, meaning Holy Saviour, but it took nearly 200 years before the first settlers arrived. These were British Puritans who landed on the island of **Eleuthera** in 1648. Having fled religious persecution in Bermuda and England, they named their new home Eleuthera after the Greek word for freedom and later settled on nearby **Harbour Island** and **Spanish Wells**. These settlements were later overtaken by a larger one on **New Providence★**, but life was harsh and the harbor at Nassau soon attracted the attentions of notorious pirates including Blackbeard and Jack Rackman who based themselves here. In the early-1700s order was restored by privateer Captain Woodes Rogers who became governor and brought the islands directly under British rule. He also set up the Bahamas Assembly, which first officially met in 1729 and has continued uninterrupted to this day. The 1780s saw another wave of settlers to the islands after the American War of Independence, when 8,000 British Loyalists fled to the Out Islands, bringing their slaves to work the

---

The Bahamian people

Most of the 300,000 Bahamians are of West African descent; their ancestors were slaves brought to work the cotton plantations until slavery was abolished in 1834. The names of many Bahamians are a clue to their past. The Gibsons are reputedly from Scotland; the Alburys, Malones and Russells are said to be Irish Loyalists and the Bethels of Eleuthera claim they arrived with the **Eleutheran Adventurers**.

HISTORY

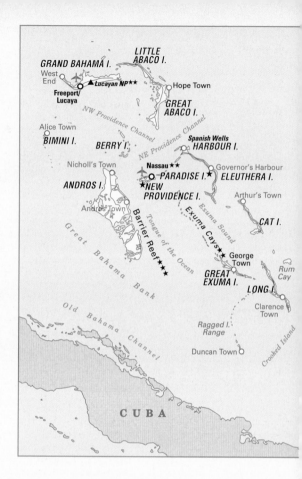

Bahamian British links

The 300 years spent under British rule are still evident in Nassau in the pretty pink Georgian buildings and the statue of Queen Victoria gazing down over Parliament Square, along with the pomp and ceremony surrounding Changing of the Guard.

cotton plantations. Many of their descendants make up a large part of the country's population today. In 1783, the Loyalists helped to drive the Spanish forces out of the entire region.

Under the colonial rule of Britain, the Bahamas went through periods of boom and bust, under the administration of a group of mainly white Bahamians called

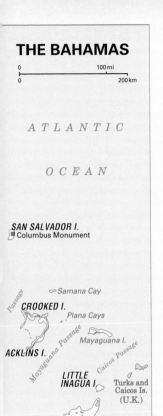

THE BAHAMAS

0 ——— 100 mi
0 ——— 200 km

A T L A N T I C

O C E A N

SAN SALVADOR I.
🏛 Columbus Monument

Samana Cay
CROOKED I.
Plana Cays
Passage
ACKLINS I.
Mayaguana Passage
Mayaguana I.
Caicos Passage
**LITTLE
INAGUA I.**
Turks and
Caicos Is.
(U.K.)
Matthew Town
**GREAT
INAGUA I.**

cessful industry the islands have ever known, contributing more than $1.4 billion a year to the economy and employing nearly 70 percent of the workforce.

The first island to be settled, **Eleuthera**, still attracts visitors, but today they are tourists and many of them head for **Harbour Island**, a ten-minute boat ride from Eleuthera's shore and famous for its **Pink Sand Beach★★** and genteel charm that makes it a magnet for celebrities.

Nearby **Spanish Wells** is unique to the Bahamas as the population is mainly white and has hardly changed over the centuries. The community still makes its living from the sea and this insular community is one of the wealthiest in the Bahamas.

Many of the inhabitants are direct descendants of the original Eleutheran Adventurers and Loyalists and still speak with traces of an old-world British accent.

The **Abacos** are the most developed of the Out Islands—the capital **Marsh Harbour** has the first and only set of traffic lights among them! They have a proud history of boat building, brought to the Abacos by the disenchanted Loyalists, which exists to this day. The superb waters surrounding the Abacos and the island's outstanding marina facilities have made them the sailing capital of the Bahamas.

Now an independent member of the British Commonwealth, the Bahamas is proud of having one of the strongest economies in the region and Bahamians take pride in their national motto: "Forward, Upward, Onward, Together."

the Bay Street Boys. But their dominance ended after World War II, a period when the country's budding tourist industry started to grow. It had enjoyed a boost during Prohibition when well-to-do Americans came to the islands but in the post-war years and after gaining independence from Britain on July 10, 1973, it continued to flourish. It is now the most suc-

NEW PROVIDENCE★: NASSAU★★

As the governmental and commercial center of the Bahamas, New Providence teems with activity. Only 22mi long and 7mi across at its widest point, New Providence is one of the smaller islands in the Bahamas, yet it is home to almost 70 percent of the country's total population. The island's historic heart, Nassau, still retains a traditional British flavor, while modern resorts rise nearby.

A Providential Place

Lucayan Indians had occupied the Bahamas for more than 500 years when **Christopher Columbus** arrived in the Caribbean in 1492. The **Lucayans**, enslaved by the Spanish to work mines on Hispaniola, were victims of disease and poor treatment. They were virtually extinct within 25 years of Columbus' arrival.

The Age of Empire – At the end of the 17th century, the British began to exercise control over the island when Proprietary Governor Nicholas Trott arrived. The settlement and its harbor soon became a center for British privateers involved in plundering Spanish and French ships in the Caribbean and for wreckers salvaging vessels that had gone down on the treacherous offshore reefs.

Grocery vendor in Nassau Dock

In the early-18th century the island's first Royal Governor, **Woodes Rogers**, transformed the rundown, garbage-strewn town of Nassau into a "civilized place." In the 1780s the modestly prospering island witnessed an influx of affluent refugees as Americans loyal to the British Crown fled the Revolution. Slaves, mostly from West Africa, were brought to work the Loyalist plantations. After slavery was abolished in 1834, free black communities turned to fishing and farming to eke out a living.

In the 1920s American Prohibition brought fleeting prosperity as local rum runners became involved in smuggling liquor to mainland bootleggers, and American gangsters and gamblers flocked to Nassau. Interest in tourism outlasted the end of Prohibition in the 1930s, resulting in the development of **Cable Beach★** as a resort area. The Bahamas gained independence from Great Britain in 1973, but traditions held over from its colonial days remain.

Today – Roughly 55 percent of visitors to the Bahamas spend time here. Nassau also ranks as a regular port-of-call for some 30 cruise ships, which deliver about a million of the roughly 4 million visitors who come to the country each year.

© The Bahamas Ministry of Tourism

30

Junkanoo

Junkanoo, a mardi-gras style festival, is said to have started in the 17th century by slaves celebrating their days off at Christmas. Slavery is a scourge of the past, but Junkanoo remains an integral part of Bahamian culture today.

Shortly after midnight on Boxing Day (December 26th), bellies full from Christmas dinner and all their presents opened, Bahamians flock to Bay Street for the first of two major parades. Groups, some with as many as a couple thousand members, 'rush' east along Bay Street, continuing the route west on Shirley Street. They compete for cash prizes that help offset the costs of creating their magical costumes and buying instruments, as well as the all important bragging rights. A week later, as soon as they've rung in the New Year, they do it all again for the second parade.

Nassau Proper

Although the name 'Nassau' is commonly used to refer to the entire island it sits on, technically, the city of Nassau is just 25 blocks bordered in the north by Nassau Harbour. The island's original tourism center runs from Bay Street in the north to East Hill Street in the south and Elizabeth Avenue in the east to the western end of West Street.

Nassau, where old world colonial charm meets modern day amenities, remains the heartbeat of the country. The streets are lined with government buildings, international banks, designer label stores and restaurants filled with locals and tourists alike. The private and public sector have accepted that Nassau, for all its charm, is in need of a makeover; plans are underway for a multi-million dollar upgrade.

Over The Hill

This area south of Nassau was created in the 1820s so that former slaves and freed Africans had somewhere to live close to work. Named for its location south of Blue Hill Road, "Over the Hill" remains a predominantly poor, but bustling with activity, neighborhood.

East & West

As you head east from the **Paradise Island★** bridges, New Providence becomes almost exclusively residential. There are shopping centers, but they serve a mostly local clientele.

Tucked amidst stately oceanfront homes is Fox Hill. Every August, this vibrant community celebrates freedom from slavery 2 weeks after the rest of the country. Apparently it took that long for news of emancipation to reach that far east.

West of Bay Street, you'll soon hit **Cable Beach★**. This is the island's other tourism hot spot.

The west, long an undeveloped pine forest with the gated community of Lyford Cay and the international airport its main points of interest, is now booming with activity.

Luxury gated communities are going up all around the economically poor but culturally rich historic settlements of Gambier Village and Adelaide.

One of particular interest is the billion dollar residential and resort development of Albany. Key investors include British multi-millionaire Joe Lewis, and golfers Ernie Els and Tiger Woods.

31

RESORTS AND SPAS

New Providence, or Nassau, as the island is more commonly referred to, has a resort to suit every style and most budgets. Whether you're looking for uninterrupted quiet at a boutique hotel, or a happening mega resort packed with activities, Nassau has it all. For more information and to find hotels not part of major resorts see *Must Stay*.

$$$$$	over $650	$$	$100–$250
$$$$	$400–$650	$	Under $100
$$$	$250–$400		

RESORTS

Graycliff

$$$$ **22 rooms**
West Hill Street, Nassau. 242-302-9150 or 1-800-476-0446. www.graycliff.com.

This historic home-turned resort in the heart of old Nassau is starting to show its age, but somehow that only adds to the old world charm. The main house, where you'll find the world famous **Graycliff Restaurant** *(see Must Eat),* lounge and a few rooms upstairs, is 260 years old.

Further rooms are situated throughout the property amid lush tropical gardens.

No two rooms are alike, but all offer views of either of two pools, the gardens, or historic Nassau. Deep below the main house lies the world famous Graycliff wine cellar. The owner will be happy to take you on a tour and show off the 250,000 bottles including a rare 1865 Château Lafite.

⛵ Marley Resort and Spa

$$$$ **16 rooms**
West Bay Street, Nassau. 242-702-2800. www.marleyresort.com.

The family of the late legendary reggae star Bob Marley have transformed their Bahamas vacation home into a chic resort and spa. Bob Marley never actually lived here, but his image and style is incorporated into every feature. If you're not a fan of The Legend, don't be scared away, it's all done in a subtle and classy fashion. The former governor's mansion is set on an idyllic stretch of **Cable Beach★**. The rooms, which bear the names of his most popular songs, are unique, some with ocean views and deep balconies, others with views of lush tropical gardens. All are furnished with Jamaican mahogany furniture and rich tapestries and linens. There are two pools sharing a deck, and the section of beach is private— unusual for a resort on Nassau.

Graycliff

© Bahamas Tourist Office

Marley Resort & Spa

© Marley Resort & Spa

On site is a small, but luxurious spa *(see p 36)*. After a day of sunning and being pampered, guests mingle with locals at the popular Stir It Up bar where they serve up Kalik and Red Stripe—the local beers of the Bahamas and Jamaica.

Compass Point

$$$ 20 rooms
West Bay Street, Nassau. 1-888-646-8721. www.compasspoint bahamas.com.

Huts, two-story cottages and cabanas are painted in bright Junkanoo-inspired colors. Rooms are large and if you open the windows, you're sure to get an amazing ocean view and breeze. Elevated cottages sit right on the

Compass Point

© Compass Point

ocean and include a private patio. There's a small beach that emerges at low tide, and guests have access to a private beach next door.
Sit in the pool or at the extra long oceanfront bar, enjoy a tropical drink and watch the spectacular Bahamian sunsets.

Sandals Royal Bahamian Spa Resort & offshore Island

$$$ 403 rooms
West Bay Street, Nassau. 1-888-726-3257. www.sandals.com. See Hotels.

This adult-only all-inclusive resort and spa offers waterscapes throughout the property with seven pools (two have swim-up bars), six whirlpools, waterfalls and a fantastic stretch of beach.
With eight restaurants on the property, you won't need to venture far from your room for a fantastic meal. There's everything from an English pub and Japanese Teppanyaki-style restaurant to elegant dining rooms offering the best in French or continental dishes with white glove service. Guests stay in the one of three clusters of rooms, each featuring different styles and amenities. For the height of luxury, make sure to book a room that comes with Rolls Royce pick up at the airport and complete butler service through-out your stay.
Sandals Royal Bahamian guests get use of the resort's private is-land just minutes offshore by ferry. There are two more beaches as well as a pool, restaurant and bar. Rates include all meals, beverages, scuba diving, watersports, airport transfer and gratuities.

RESORTS AND SPAS

33

Sheraton Nassau Beach Resort

$$$ 694 rooms

Cable Beach Strip, West Bay Street, Nassau. 242-327-6000 or 1-800-325-3535. www.starwoodhotels.com/sheraton.

Recently gutted and brought back to life, the Sheraton has also been re-named. It used to be the Sheraton Cable Beach Resort. The resort is large, but laid out in a compact design so there's not a lot of walking required.

In addition to sharing Nassau's most beautiful white sand beach with a few other resorts, The Sheraton has three pools with flowing waterfalls, oversized whirlpools, and a swim-up bar.

Rooms have all been re-designed and have either a balcony or patio giving you great views of the ocean, the pools or landscaped tropical gardens.

Enjoy free live local music every evening in the Telegraph Bar situated in the sprawling lobby. There's also free Wi-Fi in the lobby.

SuperClubs Breezes

$$$ 400 rooms

Cable Beach Strip, West Bay Street, Nassau. 242-327-5356 or 877-467-8737. www.superclubs.com.

Absolutely everything you'll need for your vacation is included in the room rate at this all-inclusive property for over 14's only.

They have all the traditional activities and watersports covered, and even have a flying trapeze set up so you can learn a few circus tricks before heading home.

There's always something going on, but there's no pressure to join in. If all you want to do is snooze on a lounge chair alongside one of the three pools or on the beautiful **Cable Beach★**, that's okay.

Rooms are simple, but comfortable, and a recent multi-million dollar renovation project included new mahogany bedroom furnishings and bathroom overhauls. Breezes Bahamas has three restaurants and three bars. There's even an on-property disco for dancing all night long.

A Stone's Throw Away

$$ 10 rooms

Located just off West Bay Street, on Tropical Garden Road & Gambier Heights. 242-327-7030. www.astonesthrowaway.com.

The main house of this boutique bed and breakfast is only four years old, but it captures the essence of an old Nassau home, complete with louvered windows and wraparound balconies.

Perched atop a limestone hillside, A Stone's Throw Away offers a magnificent view of the ocean—especially from the two top-floor suites.

Inside, rooms are luxuriously decorated in an Indonesian-Bahamian plantation-style decor.

Breakfast and lunch are served on the main deck or indoors at a large wooden dining room table. At night, guests gather in the living room for drinks. Dinner is prepared on request.

A private pool and tropical plant-covered deck overlook the surrounding Gambier neighborhood and just across West Bay Street is a lovely quiet public beach.

Just minutes away from the airport, this resort is also a perfect

Pool at A Stone's Throw Away

transit spot for guests heading on to other islands.

British Colonial Hilton

$$ **291 rooms**
Bay Street, Nassau. 242-322-9036 or 1-877-404-4586. www.hilton caribbean.com/nassau.

Situated at the head of Bay Street, The British Colonial bills itself as the businessman's hotel, but its prime location makes it a favorite with tourists seeking shopping, history and culture as well.
The BC as locals refer to it, has long been a player in Nassau's history. The original structure was built in 1900 and burned to the ground twenty years later.

A multi-million dollar renovation in the mid-1990s returned the resort to its former glory.
Rooms are spacious, nicely decorated and include separate baths and showers. There are also two executive floors complete with businessman's lounge for private meetings and quiet work.
Step outside the hotel and you're right in the midst of bustling Bay Street.
From the 300 foot private white sand beach, you can watch some of the world's largest cruise ships sail in and out of Nassau Harbour.

Wyndham Nassau Resort

$$ **850 rooms**
Cable Beach Strip, West Bay Street, Nassau. 242-327-6200 or 1-800-222-7466. www.wyndham. com/hotels/NASBS.

The towers of this mega resort on the **Cable Beach★** Strip have recently been given a paint job, making it look less like a blow up bouncy castle.
There's a 5,000 square foot fitness center overlooking the ocean, 10 restaurants and bars, and a large

British Colonial Hilton

35

pool with a waterfall and spiral water slide.

In Nassau, this is your best bet if you want to spend your days on the tees and nights on the slots. It's the only property with a casino and golf course.

The Wyndham is also a great option for a family on a budget. Kids 11 and under stay free ($4 a night gratuity for kids age 4–11).

SPAS

Natural Mystic Spa

Marley Resort, West Bay Street. 242-702-2800. www.marley resort.com.

Some of the best treatments this boutique spa has to offer take place outdoors in the secluded unique 'Wata' passage. Before lowering yourself into one of the hot or cold plunge pools, soak your worries away in a special herb bath. This is a ritual that Bob Marley's widow Rita continues to this day.

Coffee, rum or mint tea scrubs followed by the relaxing Sabai Fusion Touch massage are luxurious. Manicures and pedicures are done in an upstairs suite, with ocean views to complete the experience.

Red Lane Spa

Sandals Royal Bahamian Resort, West Bay Street. 1-888-726-3257. www.sandals.com.

This sumptuous spa has an extensive list of treatments to pamper mind, body, and spirit.

Try a Salty Margarita Scrub, where you're exfoliated with a sea salt and lemongrass mixture, have a massage in the spa, on the beach, out on a pier with waves lapping around you, or on the resort's private cay, and finish up with a mani or pedi at the Tropical Nail Bar.

For the perfect souvenir, couples can book the "In Each Other's Hands" massage.

Therapists teach you the basics, help you pick your favorite massage oils, and from there, it's practice, practice, practice.

Marley Resort & Spa

© Marley Resort & Spa

CASINOS

The arrival of casino gambling in the 1920s helped to secure the Bahamas as an early leader in the tourism industry. Today, it is a multi-billion dollar industry that lures serious gamblers over from the United States on weekend junkets, and provides a fun diversion for other tourists looking to try their luck.

Crystal Palace Casino

© Cable Beach Resorts

Crystal Palace Casino (Wyndham Nassau Resort)

Cable Beach Strip, Nassau. 242-327-6200 or 1-800-222-7466. www.wyndham.com/hotels/NASBS. Open Mon–Thu 10am–4am; Fri 10am–5am; Weekends 9am–5am.

Nassau's only casino occupies a 35,000 square foot space between the Wyndham Nassau Resort and the Sheraton Nassau Beach Resort. Originally opened in 1983, this Las Vegas style gaming mecca has kept up with the times, recently undergoing a major renovation. On the 400 coin-free slot machines you can place bets from 1¢ to $100. Or you can step your gaming up a level and try your hand at blackjack craps, roulette, Baccarat or Texas Hold Em Bonus Poker. Tucked inside the casino is the Rainforest Theatre where you are likely to catch a big name international entertainer in concert.

Locals Banned

As you're working the tables and playing slots, you may notice that the only Bahamians are dealing cards and serving drinks.

It is illegal for Bahamians or even non Bahamian residents to gamble in the casinos. That said, a blind eye is turned to other forms of gaming. Those 'web shops' found all over the island are actually numbers houses where locals place their illicit bets.

BEACHES

The best quintessential sandy white beaches in Nassau are in-accessible from land or lined with hotels and tourists. There are, however, some lovely beaches far from the crowds of the main tourist drags. It's good to know that if you can get to a beach marked 'private' without trespassing, no one can kick you off. By law, all beaches are public up to the high water mark.

Cable Beach★

West Bay Street, Nassau.

It's no surprise that some of the biggest resorts on the islands settled on this stretch of beach to set up shop. Cable Beach, so named for the underwater communications cable linking the Bahamas with the United States, is one of the more fast paced beaches, with native music pulsating from the nearby pools, jet skis and boats pulling parasails careering up and down, and women peddling T-shirts and hair braiding services.

Cable Beach

© The Bahamas Ministry of Tourism

Pleasant Bay★

Western Road, Lyford Cay.

A lovely Crescent Beach with easy public access edges the southern half of the small protected bay here, culminating in Clifton Point. The bay's northern half fronts the exclusive homes of Lyford Cay.

Adelaide Beach

Adelaide, West Bay Street.

Miles from the hustle and bustle and crowds of Nassau, you'll find this gem tucked away behind a quaint old village *(see p 47 & 51)*. At high tide, the beach is reduced to a narrow stretch of seaweed covered sand. However, at low tide the ocean recedes hundreds of feet, giving way to sand banks and rocky tide pools.
With the exceptions of Sunday afternoons and public holidays when locals crowd the beach for loud and boisterous picnics, this beach is pretty much deserted.

Saunders Beach

West Bay Street, Nassau. Opposite Shell Gas Station.

This is a popular after school, weekend and holiday spot for Bahamian families.
The beach is right along a main road, so there's not a lot of privacy, but it's a lovely beach all the same. There are tide pools to explore and the gas station across the street is a good place to pick up drinks and snacks.

HISTORIC BUILDINGS

Nassau has a colorful history dating back many centuries, and luckily, many buildings and structures have stood the ages. Historic Nassau reveals to the visitor the 'golden age' of lawless pirates and the colonial days of British influence and religion.

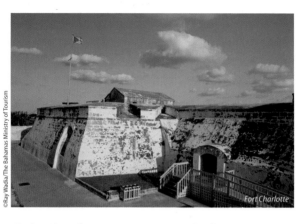

©Ray Wadia/The Bahamas Ministry of Tourism

Fort Charlotte

Christ Church Cathedral★

George Street, downtown Nassau. No admission fee.

It wasn't until Christ Church Cathedral was built in 1684 that Nassau officially became a city.

The impressive stone structure that remains today is actually the fourth cathedral to be built on this site. Previous versions were destroyed by fire, invaders from Spain and termites.

Mass is still held here and Christ Church is the setting for important state funerals and other ceremonies, including the annual opening of the Supreme Court.

The Cathedral has impressive stained glass windows and an interesting Remembrance Garden.

Fort Charlotte★

See map p 50 (C). West Bay Street across from Arawak Cay. 242-322-7500. Open daily 8am–4pm. $5.

Built to protect Nassau's harbor, Fort Charlotte was armed with iron canons, but never had to fire a shot. Built in the late-1700s, the largest of Nassau's forts remains intact, dungeons and all.

Named after King George III's consort, Fort Charlotte cost far more than anticipated to construct. Its fortified walls were carved out of solid rock.

Tour guides lead you through the moat, dungeons and underground passages, all the while spinning a tale of Nassau in the days of pirate and plunder. There's no charge, but guides, dressed in period costume, do expect a tip.

Pack a light lunch and plan to

spend a few hours sitting on the grassy hill that leads to Fort Charlotte. It's a great spot to catch some breeze and watch cruise ships and Haitian sloops sail into Nassau Harbour.

Balcony House

Market Street, downtown Nassau. 242-302-2621. Open Mon–Fri 9:30–4:30pm (Thu 1pm).
No admission fee, donations welcomed.

This Loyalist-style 18th century wooden home is thought to be the oldest one still standing in the city. It's easy to see how it got its name—the overhanging balcony is an unusual feature in old Bahamian architecture.
The pink and white house was purchased by the Central Bank of the Bahamas next door and put in trust for the Bahamian people. Today, it contains interesting historical bits and pieces as well as period furnishings and antiques. The stately mahogany staircase was salvaged from a wrecked ship centuries ago.

Cenotaph

Parliament Street, downtown Nassau. No admission fee.

This simple stone monument actually sits in the midst of the Garden of Remembrance immediately south of the Supreme Court Building.
It's easily overlooked, but worth a stop for its historic significance. Erected to honor Bahamians killed during the two World Wars, it also pays homage to the four Royal Bahamas Defence Force marines killed when their ship, the Flamingo, was attacked by Cuban fighter planes in 1980.

Fort Fincastle

Bennet's Hill, Elizabeth Avenue, Nassau. Open Mon–Fri 8am–5pm. No admission fee.

It's not clear just why this fort was designed in the shape of a paddle wheel steamer.
Fort Fincastle was built in 1793 by Lord Dunmore, Governor of the Bahamas from 1787 to 1796. It was built to protect the City of Nassau

Balcony House

as well as **Paradise Island★**, which at the time bore the less romantic name Hog Island. A light atop the fort once guided ships until the Paradise Island lighthouse was built in 1816.

Fort Montagu

Eastern Road. No admission fee.

The least impressive of Nassau's three remaining forts, Fort Montagu was built right on the water to guard the eastern entrance to the harbor from attack.
The oldest surviving fort (Fort Nassau, formerly on the site of the British Colonial Hilton was built in 1697 and demolished in 1837) was built out of limestone in 1742. You can walk inside and climb up to the deck which still houses a few iron canons.

Government House

Duke and George Streets.
242-322-2020. Closed to the public.

As a former British colony and current member of the Commonwealth, the Bahamas maintains certain traditions despite being independent since 1973.
The Governor General is the representative of Her Majesty, Queen Elizabeth II and lives in Government House. High atop a hill overlooking the old city of Nassau, Government House is a fine representation of the colonial-style architecture that helps Nassau maintain its old town feel. The property is guarded at all entrances by members of the Royal Bahamas Defence Force and is not accessible to the public. At the foot of the sprawling property sits a statue of Christopher

Columbus, who 'discovered' the New World when he landed in the Bahamas in 1492.
On the second and fourth Saturday of the month, from 10am until noon, be sure to catch the pomp and pageantry of the **changing of the guard**.

Jacaranda House

East Hill and Parliament Streets.
Closed to the public.

To get a good look at this stately historic home, you're going to have to peer through wrought iron gates on Parliament Street. Initially constructed in the 1840s by the Chief Justice of the day, it's been unoccupied but well maintained for years.
The jalousie windows and corner quoins on the southern side are typical of colonial Bahamian architecture.

Nassau Public Library

Shirley Street, between Bank Lane and Parliament Street, Nassau.
242-322-4907. Open Mon–Thu 10am–8pm (Fri 5pm; Sat 4pm).
No admission fee.

In the late-1700s, this octagonal-shaped building served as the capital's jailhouse.
Criminals now spend their time at Her Majesty's Prison in Fox Hill on the eastern end of the island, and in 1873, this building was converted into a library. It's topped by a third-floor wrap-around gallery and belfry, whose bell once summoned members to the House of Assembly.
Inside, you'll find a collection of books on the Bahamas, old maps and photographs detailing

Nassau Public Library

©Bahamas Tourist Office

significant historic events, as well as some impressive Arawak Indian artifacts.

Public Buildings

Clustered in the block encased by Bay and Shirley Streets on the north and south and Bank Lane and Parliament Street on the east and west, lie some of Nassau's historic public buildings.

Built in the early-1800s, these pink buildings with their green wooden shutters depict a Loyalist influence. If you stand in **Parliament Square** and face south, immediately ahead is the Senate.

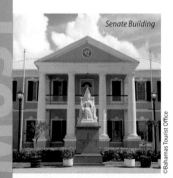

Senate Building

©Bahamas Tourist Office

This large, two story building once housed the post office, Legislative Council and court room.

The building to the east, once the Colonial Secretary's Office and Treasury, now houses court and parliamentary offices.

The **House of Assembly** (**A** on map p 48) has always occupied the westernmost building and you can go upstairs to the public gallery and watch parliamentary debates in action.

Immediately behind the Senate building is the more modern **Supreme Court** (**B** on map p 48) building which was designed in the same colonial style.

Parliament Square is also home to the **statue** (**2** on map p 48) of a serenely young Queen Victoria. Across the brick-lined section of Bay Street is Rawson Square. Locals and tourists relax on benches beneath huge shady trees. Facing the Parliament is a bronze bust of **Sir Milo Butler**, who became the first Bahamian Governor General following Independence from England in 1973.

St Andrew's Presbyterian Church

Prince's Street at Peck's Slope, Nassau. 242-322-5475.

Referred to locally as simply "The Kirk," this church, the second oldest in the country, was the first in the Bahamas to buck the Anglican tradition.

The original structure was built in 1810, but over the years, has been added to. The bell tower and other sections were built in 1864.

MUSEUMS AND GALLERIES

A growing appreciation in the Bahamas of art and culture has led to the creation of a number of galleries and museums showcasing the best examples.

National Art Gallery of the Bahamas

National Art Gallery of the Bahamas/
Bahamas Tourist Office

National Art Gallery of the Bahamas★

*West and West Hill Streets.
242-328-5800. www.nagb.org.bs.
Open Tue–Sat 10am–4pm.
$5, children 12 and under free.*

In a long overdue move, the Government of the Bahamas resurrected the dilapidated Villa Doyle mansion and established the country's first National Art Gallery. The collection includes priceless works of Bahamian artists whose works are sought by international collectors, and also showcases the best of up and coming artists. Amos Ferguson, Max Taylor, John Cox and the late Brent Malone are just some of the better known artists whose works are on display. Check the gallery's website for special exhibits and events, including summertime movies on the manicured lawn.
The gift shop is a great place to pick up some unique souvenirs.

Bahamas Historical Society

Shirley Street and Elizabeth Avenue, downtown Nassau. 242-322-4231. www.bahamashistorical society.com. Open Mon–Tue, Thu–Fri 10am–4pm, Sat 10am–noon. Closed Wed, Sun and July–August. $1.

You'll find some fascinating photographs, documents and artifacts housed in this unpretentious museum. The exhibits cover the past 500 years of Bahamian history so you get a real idea of just how much the country has changed over the years.

Bahamas Historical Society/
Bahamas Tourist Office

Bahamas Historical Society

Bahamian Heritage Centre

West Bay Street, Nassau. 242-327-8153 or 242-327-7922. www.nettiesplace.com. Open daily except Tuesday. Tours at 11am, noon & 1pm. $20, children under 16 $16. Includes brown bag lunch and drink.

Bahamian historian Nettica Symonette has a unique way of bringing the country's history to life.

MUSEUMS AND GALLERIES

Visit Granny's Kitchen and watch bread being baked in the rock oven, sit down for a game in domino square, say a prayer in the Lil Ole Chapel and listen to her weave a tale in Guamalemi Square. Symonette is also the country's local bush medicine expert.

Pompey Museum of Slavery and Emancipation

Vendue House, northwestern end of Bay Street. 242-326-2566. Open Mon–Sat 9:30–4:30pm, (Thu 1pm). $3, children under 14 $1.

Located in what was once Nassau's marketplace for the 18th and 19th century slave trade, the Pompey Museum is now dedicated to studying and depicting the history of slavery in the Bahamas. It relies mostly on articles, letters and photos from the time.
The museum, established in 1992,

was named after a maverick slave from Exuma who fought for the right for slaves in the Bahamas to be able to work part time for themselves prior to full emancipation in 1834.
It's interesting to note that the building that houses the museum is called Vendue House. "Vendue" is the French word for "sold."

PopPop Studios

26 Dunmore Avenue, Chippingham, Nassau. 242-322-7834. www.popopstudios.com. Call for opening times.

Until recently, this site was home to a guest house. Today, the main house contains artists' workshops and studios and a central gallery. Exhibits tend to be less traditional forms of Bahamian art.
Artist's talks are often held here as well. Call or check their website for a schedule.

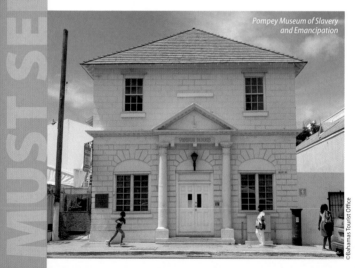

Pompey Museum of Slavery and Emancipation

©Bahamas Tourist Office

PARKS AND GARDENS

Although the island is quite developed, there are a handful of parks where you can get up close and personal with native flora and fauna. Get up early to start your adventures and you'll increase your chances of spotting birds in their natural habitats.

Botanic Gardens

West Bay Street, opposite Arawak Cay. 242-323-5875. Open Mon–Fri 8am–4pm, Weekends 9am–4pm. $1, children 50 cents.

Escape the hustle and bustle of Nassau and visit these sprawling gardens. Well maintained, but not much is marked, so unless you're an expert on Bahamian flora and fauna, it's hard to know exactly what's what.

The 18 acres includes about 600 different species of plants, trees and flowers.

There's an artificial waterfall and also a small pond in the middle of the gardens.

The covered deck overlooking the gardens is a great place to enjoy lunch, but be sure to bring one along as there is no concession stand on site.

The Botanic Gardens are completely enclosed by fences and walls, so it's a great safe place to let the kids run around and blow off some steam.

In the third weekend of October, this is the site for the annual two-day International Cultural Festival *(see sidebar below)*

Harrold and Wilson Ponds National Park

Fire Trail Road, Nassau. 242-393-1317. www.bnt.bs. Open access, no admission fee.

In an ongoing effort to protect nature in highly developed Nassau, the Bahamas National Trust officially opened the Harrold and Wilson Ponds National Park in April, 2007. The National Trust is a non-governmental, self funded, non-profit organization who want to open up this National Park to more visitors, both Bahamians and tourists. Although the actual protected area spans 250 acres, only a small section is currently accessible to the public.

A 1,000 foot wooden boardwalk and viewing platform is just the first phase of what will be a $3 million development.

More than 100 bird species have already been spotted in the park, including herons, egrets and the endangered Bahama Swallow.

International Cultural Festival

The first festival was held in 1995 to mark the anniversary of the founding of the UN, of which the Bahamas is a Member State. More than 40 countries are represented by international groups living in the Bahamas, who cook and serve food native to their countries. There's also live entertainment throughout the day, which in the past has included the National Ballet of Haiti and Scottish bag pipers. *Event held in October, for information phone 242-327-1530. Entry $2.*

The Retreat Gardens

Village Road, Nassau. 242-393-1317. www.bnt.bs. Open Mon–Fri 9am–5pm. $2, children $1.

If you want to get away from it all for a few hours, this is the place to come.

Tucked into the heart of a residential neighborhood, the aptly named Retreat is an 11-acre oasis. Inside, you'll find one of the largest and most diverse collections of **palms★** in the world—176 species. Also within are native trees including horseflesh, madeira, gum elemi, logwood, and tamarind.

Birdwatchers can get close up views of a variety of species drawn to the gardens by all the native berries.

The Retreat also doubles as the headquarters for the very active **Bahamas National Trust** *(242-393-1317, www.bnt.bs)*.

In mid-October, the gardens play host to the BNT's annual **Wine and Art Show** and in late November, the **BNT Jollification** kicks off the Christmas season with local crafts, foods, drinks and of course, Christmas music.

HISTORIC SITES

Nassau has a rich history and many of the buildings and sites have survived the ages, making it easy to take a walk through the country's history. Most sites are within walking distance of downtown Nassau.

The Caves

West Bay Street, Nassau.

These limestone caves sitting right along the main road are impressive for their historical importance, rather than as a natural feature. It was just beyond this point that US President John F Kennedy, Canadian Prime Minister John Diefenbaker, and British Prime Minister Harold Macmillan met during their 1962 Nassau summit.

The Queen's Staircase

Elizabeth Avenue, Nassau.

The '66 Steps' are thought to have been carved out of limestone in 1793 by slaves. Today, they are a busy and pretty tourist spot leading to Fort Fincastle, and in the early morning locals incorporate them into their exercise routine.

The Water Tower

Bennet's Hill, Nassau.

At 126ft, sitting high atop Bennet's Hill, the Water Tower is still the highest point in Nassau. Whether you can take the elevator up to

Natural Sites

Nassau has lots of natural sites to explore, but most are well off the beaten path. Bahamas Outdoors *(242-362-1574. www.bahamasoutdoors.com)* offers individual and group walking and bicycle tours of various habitat areas, including the National Trust nature reserves. You'll see and learn about birds, butterflies, native plants and bush medicine.

People to People

One of the best ways to experience the Bahamas is with a native. The Ministry of Tourism's People to People program has matched Bahamians and visitors for more than 30 years. Your hosts may invite you over for a home cooked dinner, give you a tour of their favorite spots or even take you to church. Whatever you do, it's sure to add a one of a kind experience to your vacation. Contact the Ministry of Tourism *(peopletopeople@bahamas.com)* ahead of your trip. *Available in Nassau/Paradise Island, Grand Bahama, Exuma, Abaco, Bimini and Eleuthera.*

The Queen's Staircase

© The Bahamas Ministry of Tourism

the top seems to be at the whim of whoever is in charge, but if it's open, go up and enjoy some of the most commanding 360-degree **views★** of the harbor and the island's interior.

Adelaide Village

Southwestern New Providence

This historic village was established in 1831 by freed black slaves, not long after the abolition of slavery. The British Royal Navy liberated the African men and women from a Portuguese vessel where they were on their way to life as slaves in the New World. Instead, the governor of the Bahamas provided them with land where they could settle.

You can visit the tiny village today and walk its narrow streets to soak up the laidback and tranquil ambience. The quiet beach nearby *(see p 38)* is usually deserted and there are a few sites of interest to explore in the village *(see p 51)*.

Arawak Cay

If you've got an adventurous culinary spirit, you simply must head to Arawak Cay for lunch or dinner. "The Fish Fry" as locals call it, is home to a smattering of shacks specializing in local treats including fried snapper, conch salad and sky juice—a potent gin and coconut water concoction infused with sweet milk and nutmeg. Some of the shacks have evolved into fancy air conditioned restaurants, and many offer native music, sometimes coming from live bands, elsewhere pumping out of stacked speakers. Watch as the professionals slice and dice conch and veggies for a bowl of fresh conch salad. *West Bay Street, Nassau.*

WALKING TOUR

Although it is typically used to refer to the entire New Providence island, Nassau is actually just the capital city running along Nassau Harbour. Originally Charles Town, it is now named after the Prince of Orange Nassau, William III of England.

OLD TOWN

▶ Begin at the intersection of West Hill St. and Cumberland St., which becomes Blue Hill Rd.

Graycliff

10 W. Hill St. (on corner of Cumberland St./Blue Hill Rd.).

This dignified Georgian Colonial Structure is one of the oldest hotels in the Bahamas.

▶ Cross Cumberland St. and walk briefly south; turn left (east) on Duke St.

Broad stone steps on the street's south side lead to Government House. A statue of **Christopher Columbus (1)**, overlooks the town.

Government House

Corner of Blue Hill Rd. and Duke St. See p 41.

▶ Continue east on Duke St. to the intersection with Market St.

Note the stone archway on the south end of the street: known as **Gregory Arch**, it was built in the 1850s and gave access to Grant's Town, one of the traditionally black "over the hill" neighborhoods.

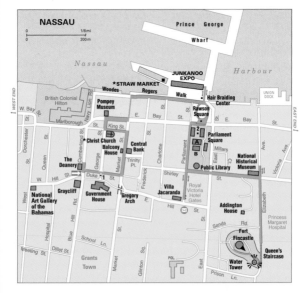

▶ Turn left on Market St. and continue one block.

Small, aptly named **Balcony House** *(Market St. and Trinity Pl.)* is over 200 years old.

▶ Continue one block north on Market to King St. Turn left on King and walk west one block to George St.

Christ Church Cathedral★

George and King Sts. See p 39.

▶ Turn right on George St. and walk one block north to Bay St.

The historical **British Colonial Hilton** anchors the north end of East Bay Street, former site of Fort Nassau (1695–1899).

▶ Cross Bay St. to north side.

Straw Market★

Bay St. across from Market St. See p 55

▶ Walk through the market to its north, waterfront side.

Woodes Rogers Walk

This walk leads along the dock area to shady **Rawson Square**.

▶ Walk south to Rawson Square and cross to south side of Bay Street.

Parliament Square

Governmental hub of the Bahamas. See p 42.

▶ Walk south up Parliament Street and turn left onto Shirley Street.

The octagonal **Nassau Public Library**, on the south edge of Parliament Square *(corner of Parliament and Shirley Sts.)*, was once the city jail.

▶ From the library, continue east on Shirley Street.

After passing the intersection *(left side)* of Millars Court, note the now overgrown expansive lawn that sweeps upward to the mid-19C **Addington House**, formerly the official residence of the Anglican Bishop of Nassau and the Bahamas.

▶ Walk east on Shirley St. to the intersection with Elizabeth St. and turn left.

National Historical Museum/Bahamas Historical Society

Northwest corner of Shirley and Elizabeth Sts. See p 43.

▶ Walk south one block along Elizabeth Street.

Climb the steep, 66-step **Queen's Staircase** which occupies a pleasant setting. The stairs are thought to have been built by slaves in the 1790s.

▶ At the top of the Queen's Staircase.

Fort Fincastle and the **Water Tower** offer spectacular **views★** for a great finish to the walk.

DRIVING TOUR

It's hard to get lost when touring Nassau as most of the key sites are on or just off the same road. Eastern Road turns into East Bay, then Bay Street, then West Bay Street, but is technically the same strip of asphalt. Remember to keep to the left side of the road. The tour is 20 miles.

▶ From the British Colonial Hotel, head west on W. Bay St. After .5mi take the unmarked road to the left at the sign for Bahamas Medical Arts Institute. Continue .3mi to the parking area for **Fort Charlotte★**.

Fort Charlotte★ (C)

On Marcus Bethel Way and West Bay Street behind Clifford Park. See p 39.

▶ Return to W. Bay St. and continue west. Turn left on Chippingham Ave. and continue .3mi. Turn right at sign for zoo.

Ardastra Gardens and Zoo (D)

Off Chippingham Avenue, just west of Botanic Gardens. See p 52.

▶ Return to W. Bay St., turn left and continue west .5mi.

Following the curve of the shoreline, you will pass **Saunders Beach**, a narrow but popular roadside beach with views out to Crystal and Long cays. After rounding Go Slow Bend, the road bends south along **Goodman's Bay**, another roadside beach. A sweeping view here scans the high rises of **Cable Beach★**.

Cable Beach★

See p 38.

▶ Continue west on W. Bay Street.

After crossing the Sandyport Bridge, the road returns to the water's edge. A pink house (private residence) hugging a point *(.8mi beyond the bridge)* is recognizable as one of the settings from the James Bond movie Thunderball. After .6mi, look to the left for **The Caves**, a limestone labyrinth once used by Lucayan Indians and now home to a colony of bats. Beyond this, the road curves past long, narrow **Orange Hill Beach.**

▶ Continue west 2mi past Blake Road.

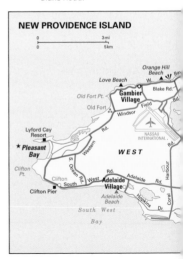

NEW PROVIDENCE ISLAND

50

Gambier Village

This hamlet is one of the oldest settlements on the island. Liberated Africans, freed from Caribbean slave ships by the Royal Navy, established Gambier Village as a farming community shortly after 1807. Recently it has become a tourist destination with the development of Compass Point.

▸ At Lyford Cay roundabout, continue south 2.5mi. Turn right at turnoff for **Pleasant Bay★**.

Pleasant Bay★

See p 38.

The dock has been reduced to pilings, but stroll along the beach that was featured in the movie Jaws.

▸ Return to the main road and head southwest about 4mi.

Adelaide Village

Wandering into this quaint village is like stepping back in time. It has a fascinating history *(see p 47)*. Pass St James Anglican Church with the bell in the yard and drive over the creek bridge. Take a left to explore the overgrown graveyard, or continue straight ahead to the beach *(see p 38)*. **Avery's Restaurant & Bar** *(242-362-1547)* is a great spot to grab a bite to eat before heading back the way you came.

©Ray Wadia/The Bahamas Ministry of Tourism

Small church in Adelaide Village

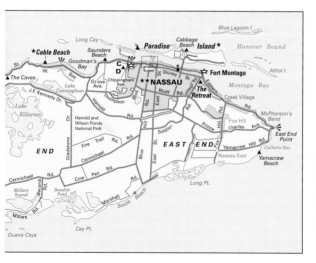

DRIVING TOUR

FOR KIDS

Just in case it's possible that the kids tire of playing in the hotel pool or seeking shells and building sandcastles on the beach, there are many other activities to keep them occupied both in and out of the water.

Ardastra Gardens

Chippingham Road, Nassau. See map p 50 (D). 242-323-5806. www. ardastra.com. Open daily 9–5pm. $15, children age 4–12 $7.50, 3 & under free.

Kids of all ages will enjoy this small zoo, home to nearly 300 mammals, birds and reptiles.
Many of the critters at Ardastra are native to the Bahamas, but there are quite a few you wouldn't expect to find on a small tropical island. There's Lulubelle, the Vietnamese pot-bellied pig who likes to lie right along the pathway near the zoo entrance, the Lory parrots you can help feed each afternoon, Madagascar lemurs, monkeys and two jaguars.
The show stealers at Ardastra are the world famous marching flamingos. They were featured in the 1957 edition of National Geographic magazine. At show time, willing kids get picked out of the crowd to join the flamingos as they pose on one leg for photos. Show times are 10:30am, 2:10pm and 4:10pm daily.
There's a small gift shop where you can pick up all sorts of Bahamian souvenirs as well as zoo inhabitant-related toys.

Dolphin Encounters

Blue Lagoon Island, just north of Nassau. 242-363-1003. www.dolphinencounters.com. Open daily, departures starting at 8:30am. Admission price varies by program.

This top rated attraction opened in 1989 with two Atlantic Bottlenose dolphins from a Nassau aquarium that was closing. Today, they have a family of 18 dolphins, five sea lions and a 325-pound loggerhead turtle named Lucky.
Three of the dolphins are real celebrities. They starred in the 1996 movie "Flipper."

Little girl swims with a dolphin

Horseback riding on the beach

Varying degrees of interaction with dolphins and sea lions are available for children as young as 3. The most popular is the Dolphin Swim *($165pp, age 6+)*. For the more timid, there's the Dolphin Encounter where you stand on a waist deep submerged platform and rub and kiss the dolphins. *($85, age 3+)*.

If sea lions are more your style, the Sea Lion Encounter gets you up close and personal for 'hand shakes' and kisses *($80, age 8+)*.

Gallop on the Beach

Happy Trails Stables, Coral Harbour, Nassau. 242-362-1820. www.windsorequestriancentre. com/trails.php. Mon–Sat, pick up between 8 and 8:30am depending on hotel. Trail rides $150pp.

Kids have to be at least 12 years old to take a horseback ride along the beach with Happy Trails Stables.

After a comprehensive introduction and basic riding instruction at the stables, you and your mount will be led through the pine forest to a secluded beach. The ride usu-ally lasts about an hour and a half. The trail ride price includes round trip bus transfer from your hotel.

Pirates of Nassau

King & George Street, Nassau. 242-356-3759. www.pirates-of -nassau.com. Open Mon–Sat 9am–6pm, Sun 9am–noon. $12, children $6.

Once upon a time, Nassau's streets and harbors were overrun with plundering pirates. Today the only place you'll find any is at the Pirate Museum.

The interactive and atmospheric museum takes you back to Nassau in the golden age of piracy. Most of the museum is an actual size ship replica, that you walk into and see, hear and smell what this tough life was really like.

The infamous Blackbeard, and some of the most fierce women of the day, Anne Bonney and Mary Reade were key players in the days of piracy.

You'll also see how Woodes Rogers came in and cleaned up the town, putting an end to the pirates' domination of Nassau.

FOR KIDS

Surrey Ride

Behind Rawson Square on Woodes Rogers Walk, downtown Nassau.

These straw hat wearing horses and their colorful fringed carriages line up in between surrey rides in a specially built rest area.

Let your kids pick their horse and carriage, then hop on for a clip-clopping slow paced ride through old Nassau.

The drivers have gone through Ministry of Tourism sponsored programs and offer their own slightly tweaked historical overviews of Bahamian history. It's a great way to see most of the sites of interest and decide which are worth a return trip for a visit.

Carriages will carry two adults and two children or three adults.

Cost for a half hour ride through the streets of Nassau is $10 per adult, $5 per child.

Most drivers will gladly take you on an extended tour if you ask before starting out.

SHOPPING

Nassau has by far the best shopping in the entire country. Its duty free designation has attracted some of the most luxurious brands found on any high street in the world. Bargaining is only done in the **Straw Market★**, and fixed prices are the same in US and Bahamian currency.

Bay Street

Downtown Nassau.

Nassau's best merchandise and deals are found in the shops lining Bay Street in historic Nassau.

Almost everything you can find in these stores is duty-free and free of sales tax, so the prices are generally lower than those you'd find for the exact same item in the United States or Europe.

Almost every other store sells jewelry, but you'll also find great deals on designer handbags, shoes, crystal and china.

Bay Street

© The Bahamas Ministry of Tourism

If you're in the market for a designer bag, make sure to buy it in one of the signature boutiques, otherwise you're likely to end up with a fake.

Be sure to pop into the arcades and peek down side streets as some of the best little gems are found off the main drag.

Straw Market★

Northwestern end of Bay Street, Downtown Nassau.

This world famous Nassau landmark lost a lot of its lustre after the actual building was destroyed by fire in 2001. Ever since, the hundreds of vendors and their wares have had to set up shop in a hot, white tent.

The Straw Market retains a true market atmosphere, with ladies yelling to get your attention and lure you over to their stall, tourists and vendors engaging in animated bartering negotiations, and kids running up and down the narrow aisles.

This is the only place where bargaining is accepted and even expected. You can usually get sellers to go down about 25% from

Straw Market, Nassau

© The Bahamas Ministry of Tourism

the original offer.

Much of the straw work on sale these days is imported from Taiwan and the vendors sew on the raffia detail. It's a great place to pick up t-shirts and sea shells. Lately, the Straw Market has become a haven for fake designer merchandise. If the price of the bag you were eyeing in a boutique up the street seems too good to be true in the market, chances are it's a knock off.

Quintessential Souvenirs

Bahama Handprints.

Island Traders Building Annex, off Mackey Street, south of Paradise Island Bridge. 242-394-4111. www.bahamahandprints.com.

Beautiful hand printed and dyed fabrics in every possible hue make these garments and home accessories special. Pick up an outfit, bag or even an apron and take a piece of the Bahamas home with you.

Cigars

Although you'll find them in abundance in Nassau, it's illegal to take Cuban stogies back home to the United States. A great alternative is the Bahiba, rolled at the Graycliff Cigar Factory just west of the stately hotel on West Hill Street *(242-302-9150)*. Cuban cigar rollers use leaves from the Dominican Republic, Honduras and Nicaragua to create a unique, award winning line of cigars.

SHOPPING

Bahama Handprints

© Bahama Handprints

Mortimer's Candy Kitchen.

East Street north, Nassau. 242-322-5230. www.mortimercandies.com.

Since 1928, this family owned candy shop has been creating colorful sweet treats. Try their soft mints, coconut cream candy, the slightly bitter benny cake or Bahamian peanut brittle. On a hot day, pop in and get a snow cone—shaved ice drenched in a super sweet syrup. Candies are pre-packaged, so pick up an assortment to take home for your friends.

My Ocean.

Charlotte Street, south of Bay Street. 242-325-3050.

Made at a nearby factory in Nassau, these soaps, scrubs, lotions and candles are infused with the smells and colors of the islands.

The Island Bookstore

Bay Street, Nassau. 242-322-4183.

The big draw is the second floor bookshop which has a Bahamian books section, with everything from history to cookery.

OUTDOOR SPORTS

Golf is a popular activity with tourists and locals alike, but there is only one public course in Nassau—the Lyford Cay course is members only. There's been talk of the South Ocean golf course re-opening soon, which local putters say is by far the best course on the island.

Golf

**Cable Beach
Golf Course**

West Bay Street, Cable Beach, Nassau. 242-327-6000.

This really is your only option for golfing on Nassau. Although it's not a championship course, it does offer some good challenges for even the serious golfer. The 7,040 yard, par-72 course has lakes and ponds and is cut in half

Live Sports

Connie and Chris Robertson run the friendly Cricket Club Restaurant and Pub, open 7 days a week. On weekends, watch all the action from the balcony overlooking the Bahamas cricket ground. If wickets aren't your thing, this is still the place to watch any of the sports from back home that you might otherwise miss out on. With the New York Knicks on the big screen and British and Bahamian fare on the menu, you'll never want to leave. *Haynes Oval. West Bay Street. Nassau. 242-326-4720. www.bahamascricket.com.*

Cable Beach Golf Course

© Cable Beach Golf Club

by a main road. A golf cart crossing makes access easy enough. The course is situated right at the eastern start of the **Cable Beach★** strip, but is across West Bay Street from the beach and ocean, so you won't have scenery to distract you. There's a driving range and putting green, and local pros lead golf clinics.

The pro shop is fully stocked with everything you need for sale or rent, so there's no need to lug your irons along.

If you want a prime tee-off time, be sure to book in advance. If you think you can handle the scorching afternoon sun, inquire about discounts for afternoon tee times.

Horseback Riding

Happy Trails Stables

Coral Harbour, Nassau. See p 53.

Fancy a morning riding through the woods and on beautiful unspoiled beaches? This riding facility offers leisurely horseback riding trails for anyone regardless of their experience. See Musts for Kids for more details.

Segway Tours

If you want to get outdoors but don't want to exert too much energy, Segway Bahamas is just the ticket. You'll take a guided tour on one of their neat personal transportation devices through a 162 acre nature preserve not far from Nassau's main drag. As you go along, your guide will point out local flora and fauna, give you a cultural and historical overview of the island and take you through a fun obstacle course. Along the way you'll stop off at a local spot where you can buy a cool drink or snack before continuing on. *Tours last about 1 ½ hours and operate 7 days a week from 8am till dusk. Minimum age is 10 and there's a 275lb weight limit. $75 per person includes ground transportation to and from hotel or cruise ship dock. Call 242-467-8764 or 242-466-7696 for reservations.*

OUTDOOR SPORTS

WATERSPORTS

With crystal clear waters and ocean temperatures that barely dip below bath tub comfort even in the winter, watersports are big business. There are lots of different ways to take advantage, both in, on and hovering high above Nassau's aquamarine ocean and white sand beaches.

America's Cup Sailing

Nassau. 242-363-1552. www.sailnassau.com. $125, children age 7–12 $85.

Spend a day learning how to sail one of two former Team New Zealand sailboats. The boats are 76ft long, have 115ft high masts and are made of high tech carbon fiber. In other words, they're built for speed. Once you and your crew have the basics down, you'll face off against another team in a mock race in open water off the coast of **Paradise Island★**. No prior sailing experience is necessary.

Big Game Fishing

The Bahamas is a huge destination for Big Game Fishing. While the Bimini Islands are considered *the* destination for competitive fishermen, roughly 55 percent of all visitors come through Nassau,

so it's no surprise to find plenty of charter options here too. Chartering your own boat does not come cheap, and you can expect to pay around $600 for half a day, and double this for a full day out on the water. On the upside, this price can often be for a group of up to 6 people. Be sure to check this includes an experienced sea captain, and all tackle, bait and ice.

Born Free Charters

Nassau. 242-393-4144. www.bornfreefishing.com.

Out on the ocean you might catch dolphin (as they point out, not our favorite porpoise flipper, but a colorful fish), wahoo, kingfish, marlin, sailfish and tuna. They have a 'No fish, no pay' policy for their full day trips. You can take the family and perhaps choose to include some snorkeling.

Fishing Calendar

Bonefish	Good to excellent year round
Kingfish	Good all year
Tuna (3 species)	March–July
Sailfish	April
Shark	April–June
Grouper	April–September
Snapper	April–September
White Marlin	May
Blue Marlin	May–June
Barracuda	June–August
Swordfish	June–September
Wahoo	November–March

Diving with sharks

© Stuart Cove's Dive Bahamas

Diving

Bahama Divers, East Bay Street, Nassau. 242-393-6054. www.bahamadivers.com; Stuart Cove's Dive Bahamas, South Ocean, Nassau. 242-362-4171. www.stuartcove.com.

In the water surrounding Nassau you'll find a fascinating array of coral reefs and wrecks to choose from.

Some of the most popular dive sites include **The Twin Sisters**—a pair of 200 foot oil tankers lying 70ft below the surface; the **Lost Blue Hole**, about 10 miles east of the mainland, 100ft in diameter with spectacular sites and sea creatures at varying depths; and **Schoolhouse Reef**, a shallow spot (15ft) with an amazing selection of fish hanging around massive coral heads.

Gouldings Cay, a tiny, uninhabited island off the southwestern coast of Nassau offers acres of diving options including amazing coral reefs and the **Tears of Allah** wreck from the James Bond flick *Never Say Never Again*.

Although the ocean around Nassau is relatively shallow, it's just a short boat ride from the northeastern wall of the **Tongue of the Ocean**, a 6,000 foot deep drop-off that separates Nassau from Andros.

For the truly adventurous, there are **Shark Dives** where you swim freely in the wild surrounded by these beautiful, if not a little intimidating, creatures. In Nassau there are a choice of dive operators all offering slightly different shark encounters. We recommend Stuart Cove's *(see p 61 for contact details)* who offer diving alongside shark awareness programs.

Jet Skis, Parasails & Banana Boat Rides

Cable Beach, Nassau.

You'll have to head to the beach lined with resorts to find these lively watersports. Operators and their operatives walk the beach seeking customers, or you can walk up and negotiate your price. Watersports operators are all regulated by government and the operators have undergone stringent training to ensure safety. Generally, children must be accompanied by an adult on jet

Parasailing

© The Bahamas Ministry of Tourism

skis. The banana boat ride, a long yellow inflatable tube towed by speed boat is a thrill-seeking ride. For the truly adventurous, opt for a parasail ride and see the sites of Nassau from a most unique perspective.

Kiteboarding

Cross Shore, Nassau.
242-393-3261 or 242-422-0756.
www.cross-shore.com.

Aussie transplant AJ Watson realized that the cool breeze that cuts across the water beyond Nassau's "Go Slow Bend" would be perfect for kiteboarding and started a hot new trend.
Classes for beginners who want to learn how to ride the water include all equipment, pick up and drop off at hotel, instruction and jet ski support.
There are packages for intermediate and experienced kiteboarders as well as multiple day excursions to the Family Islands for a change of scenery.

Snorkeling

The many pristine coral reefs dotting the shores around Nassau make it a great destination for snorkeling. Many resorts have kiosks where you can use or rent all the gear you need to see fish, sea fans and coral heads up close. To view wrecks and reefs further out to sea you can charter a boat, or for the less moneyed, book a snorkel trip.

Flying Cloud

Nassau. 242-363-4430.
www.flyingcloud.info.

The crew of the Flying Cloud add to the experience with a catamaran cruise to an active reef off nearby Rose Island.
All equipment is provided and instruction and a buddy system is offered if needed, as well as a complimentary rum punch! If the weather conditions are good then you'll drop anchor at the picturesque and secluded beach. Weekday 3½ hour tours are $60 pp and Sundays they offer a 5 hour trip that includes lunch for $75 pp.

Stuart Cove's Snorkel Bahamas

South Ocean, Nassau.
242-362-4171 or 800-879-9832.
www.stuartcove.com

Twice-daily trips are approximately 5 hours and take in 3 sites, including an optional snorkel with Caribbean Reef Sharks. If you opt out, you can still see all the action from the safety of the boat! You will be collected from your hotel or cruise ship and driven the 30 minutes to the southwest of New Providence Island, where the boat departs.

A typical trip will take in a shallow reef and a shipwreck, as well as watching shark feeding time. You are also given time to browse the on-site shop. All equipment is included in the price of $48 for adults and $30 for children age 4–11 (price is more if you don't pre-book).

Undersea Adventure

Stuart Cove's Dive Bahamas, South Ocean, Nassau. 242-362-4171 or 800-879-9832. www.stuartcove.com.

You don't have to be a master scuba diver or even a strong swimmer to experience the magic beneath the Bahamian ocean. In fact, with Stuart Cove's Sub Bahamas, you don't even have to get your hair wet. These self-contained underwater motorcycle contraptions have a clear two foot dome that covers your head, so you breath normally as you would on land. Sub dives go no deeper than 20ft, and are open to anyone age 12 and up.

Stuart Cove's SUB Bahamas trip

© Stuart Cove's Dive Bahamas

Snorkeling for all

©The Bahamas Ministry of Tourism

NIGHTLIFE

There's more to Nassau's nightlife than your hotel lobby bar. Some have created a European rave atmosphere while others stick with down home tropical appeal. There are likely to be new hot spots when you visit, as the Nassau club scene tends to be transient at best. The following places have stood the test of time.

Bambu

Corner of Charlotte Street and Woodes Rogers Walk, Nassau. Open 9pm–5am. No cover charge.

If it didn't have a pretty good view of Nassau Harbour, you may have a few too many and think you've somehow teleported into a house disco somewhere in Europe. The music ranges from top 20 to Euro Trance and there's usually a good crowd on the dance floor. Popular with younger locals and cruise ship visitors and crew, this hot spot doesn't get going until well after midnight. Of course that means the party here goes on until 4 or 5 in the morning.

Club Waterloo

East Bay Street, Nassau. 242-393-7324. Open Tue–Sat 8pm–4am. Cover charge $20. www.clubwaterloo.com.

Nightclubs in Nassau come and go. But not Club Waterloo. It's been a must do on the late night party scene for almost 30 years. This large, open air club has two dance floors, six bars, a pool and overlooks a lake.
Music ranges from reggae and calypso to techno and rock n roll, and on Friday and Saturday nights they have local bands on stage. Thursday is Ladies night and women get in free; men who show up before midnight pay just $10.

Flamingo

East of British Colonial Hotel, downtown Nassau. Open Wed–Sat, 9pm–late. No cover charge.

This little bar and smokers' room comes alive at night with live Cuban music. The indoors is tiny, so the party spills outside onto the sidewalk which is covered with a tent if rain is expected. A good place to get warmed up for the late-night club scene.

Fluid Lounge & Nightclub

King's Court Building, Bay Street south, Nassau. 242-356-4691. www.clubfluidbahamas.com. Open Wed–Sat 9pm–until late. Cover charge varies.

As you shop along Bay Street by day, you'll probably walk right past the entrance to this underground

Variety of cocktails on offer in Nassau

© The Bahamas Ministry of Tourism

Nighttime entertainment in Nassau

club. At night, bouncers and clubbers gather around so you'll know just where to go.

Nassau's hottest DJ's keep the vibe pulsing all night long with the best reggae, hip hop, soca and R&B tunes.

In addition to three full service bars, there's a beer only bar and a large dance floor.

Thursday nights ladies drink free until 1am.

If you want to escape the crowd you can always buy a pricey bottle of your favorite brand and gain access to the VIP/Bottle Lounge. Management maintains a strict dress code. They've only recently started letting men wear shorts inside.

Green Parrot Bar & Grill

East Bay Street, just west of the bridge to Paradise Island, Nassau. 242-322-9248. www.greenparrot bar.com. Open daily until 1am. No cover charge.

More restaurant and bar than nightspot, Friday's all-night happy hour has made this a favorite pre-club meeting spot for locals and tourists alike.

Saturday nights you can enjoy a live band playing everything from local favorites to Jimmy Buffett. Overlooking Nassau Harbour and **Paradise Island★**, this is a great spot to grab a light bite to eat.

Senor Frogs

Woodes Rogers Walk, downtown Nassau. 242-323-1777. www.senor frogs.com/bahamas/index.htm.

Situated right on the harborfront, Senor Frogs offers a lively combination of food, drinks and fun entertainment.

Multiple bars serving all sorts of exotic concoctions, an energetic DJ who keeps the party going, and a basic rule that there are no rules makes this a popular nightspot particularly with the 20-something tourists. Throughout the night you'll have a chance to play silly games, wow the crowd with your karaoke skills (or plug your ears as others take the mic) and dance to the hottest local and international tunes. The restaurant opens at 11am and stays open until at least 1am, making it a great spot to get the night started.

NIGHTLIFE

PARADISE ISLAND ★

This 680 square mile island joined to **Nassau**★ by two bridges, has come a long way since its early days as Hog Island. This high energy, packed with things to do resort island has earned the name Paradise.

Hog Island to Paradise

As you drive over the bridge to Paradise Island and get your first true glimpse of this resort destination, it's hard to imagine that just 40 years ago, it was for the most part, an uninhabited bush and casuarina tree covered cay.
Back then, it was known as Hog Cay, supposedly named by Governor Nicholas Trott after his father's estate in Hog Bay, Bermuda. Early in the 20th century, wealthy Americans established a winter colony of vacation homes here. The island's quiet tenor remained unchanged until 1959 when American grocery heir and philanthropist Huntington Hartford bought a large parcel of land on the island. He was determined to develop the resort potential he saw in the small island, and successfully petitioned the government of the day to change the

> ### Getting There
> A water taxi ($6 return) runs year-round between Paradise Island and **Nassau**★ (times vary, depending on demand). The Bridge is $2 (incoming only) for rental cars and taxis.

name to Paradise Island. Though Hartford's endeavors failed financially, he started the ball rolling. In 1967, the first bridge was built, connecting the island to **Nassau**★. The second was built in 1999. Various tourism moguls have had a hand in Paradise Island's development, including Donald Trump and the late Merv Griffin, but it was South African tourism and development mogul Sol Kerzner who had the vision to bring it to where it is today. His sprawling Atlantis resort and other endeavors occupy most of Paradise Island.

Aerial view of Paradise Island harborside

© Pam Mclean/Atlantis

RESORTS AND SPAS

Most of the real estate on Paradise Island has been taken up by the many glitzy resorts. You'll find all the things you need to make a fantastic vacation right here—beaches, golf, casinos, shops, restaurants, tennis, watersports. In fact, many visitors come to Paradise Island and never cross the bridge again until it's time to go home. For more information and to find hotels not part of major resorts see *Must Stay*.

$$$$$	over $650	$$	$100–$250
$$$$	$400–$650	$	Under $100
$$$	$250–$400		

Paradise Island's East Beach

© Macduff Everton/Atlantis

RESORTS

The Cove and The Reef

$$$$$ 600/497 rooms
Casino Drive, Paradise Island.
242-363-6900 or 1-877-268-3847.
www.thecoveatlantis.com.

The newest additions to Kerzner's Paradise Island resort offering, The Cove and Reef are in a class of their own. The 600-room, all suite Cove tower and the 500-room Reef, a condotel, opened in late 2007. Both are attached to the main Atlantis property, so guests can easily take advantage of all the amenities the megaresort has to offer, yet access to the beach, waterscape and certain amenities attached to these two properties is restricted to their guests, creating an air of exclusivity.

The suites at The Cove and the condos at The Reef leave nothing to spare when it comes to luxurious living. In The Reef, suites have complete kitchens or fully stocked

Ocean Delux Suite, The Reef Atlantis

© Ron Starr/Atlantis

65

Pool at Cain at The Cove

© Dana Neibert/Atlantis

kitchenettes as well as private laundry facilities.

Views from the upper floors of both towers are stunning, whether the room and balcony overlook the Atlantic Ocean or the Harbor. When it comes to Atlantis, it's hard to pick just which tower or hotel to stay in. The Cove does have one feature that's reserved exclusively for it guests and it is a pretty fabulous spot. Cain at the Cove is an ultra exclusive adult only pool area surrounded by private cabanas that open to the pool on one side and the beach just a step away on the other. From morning 'til night, a DJ keeps the mellow vibe going strong.

Beach at One&Only Ocean club

© J.Yeo/One&Only Resorts

One&Only Ocean Club

$$$$$ 114 rooms
Ocean Club Drive, Paradise Island. 242-363-2501 or 1-800-321-3000. www.oneandonlyresorts.com.

The Ocean Club sets the standard on Paradise Island for luxurious elegance. Overlooking **Cabbage Beach★**, it's far enough away from all the other resorts and public beach access walkways that it's able to maintain a level of seclusion even on this miles-long stretch of sand.

Rooms have large balconies overlooking the ocean or the lush tropical gardens and are extravagantly decorated with all the amenities you'd expect of a world class resort.

For the ultimate in privacy, opt for a 3 or 4-bedroom villa that comes with its own private infinity pool. Besides the opulent settings, the Ocean Club takes service to a whole new level, offering guests round the clock personalized butler service, fresh fruit in room every day, nightly turndown service, shoe shines and maid service twice a day.

You may recognize the Ocean Club from scenes of James Bond's *Casino Royale*.

© Tim Aylen/Atlantis
Atlantis Royal Towers at night

Atlantis Resort

$$$$ 2,327 rooms
Paradise Island. 242-363-3000 or 1-888-528-7155. www.atlantis.com.

The towering Atlantis Resort with its suspended $25,000 a night Bridge Suite has become a landmark, dominating Paradise Island and Nassau's landscapes. Atlantis, credited with turning around a slumping Bahamian tourism product when it was created in 1994 by Sun City hotelier Sol Kerzner, has become a destination in itself.

Part mega-resort, part water theme park, Atlantis has something to appeal to everyone unless you're looking for absolute solitude.

With more than 2,000 rooms in three towers—The Royal Towers, Coral Towers and Beach Towers — there's always going to be someone around. Still, despite its overwhelming size, there's enough pool and beach space that you'll be able to secure a quiet spot if that's what you're looking for. Meandering throughout the resort is the world's largest outdoor saltwater aquarium. More than 50,000 marine animals call the resort home.

Atlantis has all sorts of activities that appeal specifically to kids. There's a movie theater, Aquaventure *(see p 74)*, kids only swimming pools for the little ones, sea creatures at every turn, a pottery design studio, swimming with dolphins, Atlantis Kids Club, a nightclub exclusively for teens and tweens, a video game arcade, a remote control car speedway, and even a fish feeding program designed just for them.

There's just as much, if not more, to keep the grown ups occupied. Atlantis is home to Paradise Island's only casino *(see p 69)*, more than 35 restaurants and bars, the hippest nightclub in town, a lavish spa, a state of the art fitness center with yoga pavilion and lap pool, tennis, golf, top billing artists in concert, two beaches and pools everywhere you look.

Riu Paradise Island

$$ 379 rooms
Casino Drive, Paradise Island. 242-363-3500. www.riu.com.

The Riu is right next door to the sprawling Atlantis megaresort, but with no other properties on its eastern side, guests have a greater portion of **Cabbage Beach★** for pursuing favorite beach activities. The 14-story high rise resort is one of only a handful of all-inclusives in the Bahamas and rates include all meals, snacks, drinks, activities, entertainment, taxes, and gratuities. During the day, you can lounge by the large pool and Jacuzzi, pick a quiet spot on the world famous beach or participate in the many

Yoga Retreat

Yoga enthusiasts flock to Paradise Island not for the glitz and glamor, but for the spartan Sivananda Yoga Retreat *(242-363-2902 or 1-800-441-2096. www.my-yoga.net)*. The inexpensive rooms are as basic as you can get, but they do overlook Paradise Beach. Twice daily 2-hour meditations and 2-hour yoga classes are mandatory. There are no televisions, radios, phones or even coffee allowed.

Ocean Club Spa

Ocean Club Drive, Paradise Island. 242-363-2501 ext. 64808. www.oneandonlyresorts.com.

Whether you opt to have your treatment in your room, or in one of the 8 Balinese-style private treatment villas with waterfall showers and Jacuzzi tubs that open up to private gardens, you are bound to be pampered like never before at the Ocean Club Spa.

activities offered by the resort. At night, wander just a few hundred feet over to the Atlantis casino or stay on property and enjoy live music at one of the bars, or even a show.

SPAS

Mandara Spa

Between Royal Towers and The Cove, Atlantis. 1-242-363-3000 or 1-800-285-2684. www.atlantis.com.

The 11,500-square-foot Mandara Spa is a true sanctuary in the midst of the busy comings and goings of the resort. This Indonesian-inspired spa is full service, offering everything from the expected massage, facial and hair and nail treatments to a private sunning deck and a mens' barber shop.

Before you get started with your treatments of choice, enjoy the Taking of the Waters—warm and cold plunge pools and steam and sauna rooms separated by gender.

Spa at One&Only Ocean Club

©Bruce Wolf/One&Only Resorts

The Bahamian Pathway to Radiance is sure to re-energize and rejuvenate. It begins, as do all the special packages, with a floral foot wash ritual. From there, you are treated to the Elemis Exotic Hand Ritual, Caribbean Coffee Body Scrub, the One&Only Massage and a Reflexology Massage. Following these 30 minutes of pure bliss, enjoy the exotic Japanese Tea Ceremony.

PARADISE ISLAND

MUST SEE

CASINOS

Casino gambling first arrived on Paradise Island in 1967, soon after the island had been earmarked as the next great tourist destination. Today, the Atlantis casino is still a major draw for serious gamers and those simply eager to try their luck.

🎰 Atlantis Casino

Atlantis, Paradise Island.
242-363-3000 or 1-800-528-7155.
www.atlantis.com.

The centerpiece of Atlantis' land based features, the Atlantis Casino brings true Las Vegas style glitz and glamor to Paradise Island. The 50,000 square foot gaming facility is the largest in the Caribbean and you have a choice of more than 850 slot machines and 78 table games.

Whether you're into roulette, poker, craps, baccarat or blackjack, they've got it covered. There's also a Pegasus Race and Sports Book, the only one in the country. Tucked away behind the main gaming table area is a high roller's section. The bets are higher here and you'll often spot Hollywood celebrities trying their hand. If you've never tried gambling and want to give it a go during your Bahamas vacation, sign up for the gaming lessons held daily in the Atlantis Casino.

Cain at The Cove

The Cove, Atlantis. Paradise Island.
242-363-6900 or 1-877-268-3847.
www.thecoveatlantis.com.

This extension of the Atlantis Casino offers a new twist on gaming. Often, diehards miss out on the sun, sand and sea, opting to spend their days and nights inside the Casino. Well over at Cain at the Cove, they have an outdoor gambling pavilion right next to the pool. It's tables only—six black-jack and one mini-craps table—and as with the rest of this facility, is accessible only to registered guests.

Slot machine in Atlantis Casino

©Ron Starr/Atlantis

BEACHES

Without a doubt, the best beaches in the **Nassau★** area are found on the northern edge of Paradise Island. The two main beaches, although equal in their natural beauty, couldn't be further apart in atmosphere, one tranquil and serene, the other often crowded with jet skis offshore and calypso music coming from nearby hotels.

Cabbage Beach★

Paradise Island.

This 2 mile stretch of beach is lined by resorts and multi-million dollar homes, and is the most popular beach with tourists and locals. Hundreds of deck chairs and swimmers dot the beach and ocean on the western end, but wander further east and you'll discover the solitude you desire. Boats and watersports are kept hundreds of feet out to sea, so it's safe for swimming.

There is a slight drop off at points, so weak swimmers should stay close to the shore, and at various points along the coastline, particularly just east of the Riu Hotel, there's a strong undertow during the winter months, that sends waves, and sometimes unsuspecting swimmers, tumbling onto the shore.

If you're staying at one of the resorts lining Cabbage Beach, you'll have direct access. Otherwise, there are two public access walkways, one east of the Riu Hotel and the other just west of the Ocean Club Estates entrance.

Paradise Beach

Paradise Island,
behind The Cove and The Reef.

Since the development of The Cove and The Reef, access by land has been pretty much cut off for everyone except hotel guests and the handful of homeowners who live on the western end of Paradise Island. This tranquil beach is worth reaching. The only sounds you'll hear are seagulls and gently lapping waves.

Paradise Beach is nice and flat, great for pre-dawn power walks or romantic sunset strolls.

Cabbage Beach

©Caren Dissinger/Bahama Ministry of Tourism

HISTORIC BUILDINGS AND GARDENS

This small island has an interesting history taking it from Hog Island to Paradise, and some of the most interesting features have been lovingly maintained and worked into the modern setting.

©Ramunas Bruzas/Dreamstime.com

Cloisters

The Lighthouse

Western point, Paradise Island. Inaccessible by land.

One of the first sites seen by cruise ship visitors as they pull into Nassau Harbour, this lighthouse on the western tip of Paradise Island is now on automatic pilot. It was built out of limestone blocks quarried nearby in 1816 and to this day, the 216 foot high white lighthouse marks the entrance to Nassau Harbour.

Versailles Gardens

Paradise Island Drive.

It was A&P heir Huntington Hartford who transformed the exclusive Hog Island into Paradise Island when he spent millions to convert his private homestead into what is now The Ocean Club. He created the exquisitely manicured terraced lawns of Versailles Gardens and erected bronze statues, including two of his heroes, Franklyn D. Roosevelt and David Livingstone. Make sure to check in with the security booth before strolling the quarter mile-long gardens.

Cloisters

Paradise Island Drive.

American publishing magnate William Randolph Hearst imported this delicately styled square of archways and columns from a monastery in France. Years later, Huntington Hartford brought the stones, which were still packed in crates, and reconstructed the 14th century monastery remains on their new home at the top of Versailles Gardens. Overlooking Nassau Harbour, the Cloisters now serves as a popular site for weddings.

SHOPPING

Some of the best shopping is found on Paradise Island. Regardless of whether your idea of the perfect souvenir is a new piece of dazzling jewelry, a painting by a local artist to hang on your wall back home or a hand-made straw bag designed by a local artisan, you'll find it here.

Sollomon's Sea Treasures, Marina Village
© Tom Aylen/Atlantis

Marina Village

Parallel to the Atlantis Marina, Paradise Island.

High street meets dock side at Marina Village. Boutiques selling priceless jewels, designer hand-bags, crystal, watches and elegant or resort attire are interspersed with kiosks selling more whimsical bits and pieces.

Be sure to pop into **Doongalik Studios** *(242-363-1313)*. It's the only art gallery on Paradise Island and features some incredible works by established Bahamian artists. **The Plait Lady** *(242-363-1416)* is chock full of exquisite local crafts, including straw items that are hand made in the various islands of the Bahamas.

Crystal Court

Near the casino, Royal Towers, Atlantis. Shops open until 11pm.

The very finest is available in the trendy designer shops lining Atlantis' Crystal Court.
Thanks to the Bahamas duty free shopping, you'll find great deals on men's and women's high fashion, jewelry, cigars, and the latest lines put out by some of the world's most fashionable designers.

Earth & Fire

Beach Tower, Atlantis. 242-363-3000 ext. 64470. Open daily 10am–6pm.

What better souvenir than one you make yourself? Atlantis' own pottery shop has a large selection of Bahamian-inspired pieces to choose from. All you have to do is put on an apron, pick your color palette and start creating your masterpiece.
Your creation will be ready for pick up after 4pm the following day.

Piranha Joe, Marina Village
© Tom Aylen/Atlantis

OUTDOOR SPORTS

In addition to being a water lover's playground, Paradise Island has the best in land-based activities. Golf and tennis have long been favorites for those wanting to work off decadent vacation meals. Paradise Island is well lit and has wide sidewalks, perfect for power walks.

One&Only Ocean Club Golf Course

©John Henebry/One&Only Resort

Golf

Ocean Club Golf Course

Eastern tip of Paradise Island. 242-363-3000. Open only to guests of Ocean Club or Atlantis.

Cross winds, and a fantastic design makes this a challenging course to play, and stunning views of the Atlantic provide distraction for even the most focused golfer. This 18-hole, par-72 course was designed by legendary golf pro Tom Weiskopf and has consistently landed on Conde Nast Traveler and Golf Digest lists of the best courses in the world. The 18 holes cover 7,100 yards of Paradise Island's eastern tip and are now surrounded by the multi-million dollar homes of Ocean Club Estates.

There's a pro shop and clubhouse on site, and on course beverage cart service completes the experience. Book lessons or tee times up to 60 days in advance.

Tennis

Most of the large resorts are equipped with tennis courts and equipment rental facilities. Court time can run around $20 for an hour of play.
The Ocean Club has 6 Har-Tru clay courts, but only guests staying there can use them.
At Atlantis, where the fitness center includes 5 clay courts, you can sign up for lessons with the resident pro ($70 for an hour) or for one of the clinics. They offer junior and adult clinics for all levels of play.

73

WATERSPORTS

There are so many ways to enjoy the water on Paradise Island—take a swim in the Atlantic, lounge by one of the seemingly endless selection of freshwater pools, interact with dolphins, or take the plunge on an exhilarating ride through an acrylic tube surrounded by sharks.

Aquaventure at Atlantis

Atlantis, Paradise Island. 242-363-3000. Free for Atlantis, The Cove & The Reef guests. Non guests: $105, children 4–12 $70.

Aquaventure is 141 acres of pure water-based fun.

It was with the addition of this incredible waterpark, that Atlantis became more than an ordinary hotel.

Guests can spend the day exploring the many different features. There's a kiddie pool area for little ones not big enough to go on the rides.

The Lazy River Ride takes you on a slow, meandering journey through the park via inner tube. Those seeking more thrill than chill can choose the mile-long Current, which includes an intersection that can take you and your inner tube up a conveyor belt to the top of the Power Tower for the ride of your life.

From the top of the Power Tower, where, incidentally, you have some spectacular views of the entire property, you pick from one of four slides on two levels. There's The Falls, The Drop, The Surge and The Abyss, with its 50-foot near vertical drop at the start that will have you holding your breath for the entire 14 second thrill ride.

For more rides and slides, visit the top of the Mayan Temple, where you can take The Leap of Faith—a 60 foot near vertical plunge through a clear acrylic tunnel submerged in a shark-filled lagoon.

Bananaboats, Jet Skis & Parasails

One of the best ways to get a good view of the entire sprawling Atlantis resort and the rest of Paradise Island is strapped into a

Mayan Temple, Atlantis

© Atlantis Core Select Images/Bahamas Tourist Office

parasail. Most operators now have launch and land platforms on the back of their speedboat so you don't even have to get wet. Jetskis and banana boat rides are always a popular activity, and operators walk up and down **Cabbage Beach★** offering half hour rides. Government has recently regulated the watersports industry, bringing an added level of safety.

Dolphin Cay

Atlantis, Paradise Island. 242-363-3000. www.dolphincay atlantis.com. Price depends on program.

©Ron Garrison/Atlantis
Dolphin Cay

Dolphin Cay was born in the aftermath of Hurricane Katrina. Marine Life Oceanarium in Gulfport, Mississippi was completely destroyed, and Atlantis provided their dolphins with a new, state of the art home.

Since then the Dolphin Cay population has expanded with the birth of two calves, born to Katrina survivors Kelly and Michelle. They've also recently added some sealions to the family and offer interaction experiences with them. The dolphin facility covers 14 acres and contains more than 7 million gallons of water.

Dolphin Cay offers a shallow water interaction, where you can glide alongside a dolphin using a hand-held water scooter and then be propelled along the lagoon by dolphin power.

For a truly unique experience, sign up for the 6 hour Trainer for a Day program. You'll spend a day working with one of the marine mammal specialists, feeding, training and caring for dolphins and sea lions.

Power Boat Adventures

242-363-1466. www.power boatadventures.com. $199, children $140.

This amazing excursion actually takes you far away from Paradise Island for the day.

The beautiful **Exuma Cays★★** are just 55 minutes away when you're traveling in one of their 1,000 horsepower speedboats.

The first stop is Allan's Cay which is home to a friendly group of iguanas. As they hear the boats approaching, they waddle down to the shore and you can feed them grapes.

Next stop is Ship Channel Cay where you'll spend the rest of the day. There's lunch, shark and stingray feeding and an open bar all day long.

There's also an overnight adventure that allows you to sleep in absolute comfort on this deserted island. The two-room cottage sleeps four.

WATERSPORTS

NIGHTLIFE

Whether you're up for dancing at a club until the sun comes up, side splitting laughter at a comedy club, sipping martinis in an upscale bar or experiencing Bahamian culture up close, Paradise Island's nightlife has something for every whim and fancy.

Aura

Adjacent to the casino, Atlantis, Paradise Island. Open 9:30pm–late. Admission fee varies.

Aura has brought a certain level of coolness to Atlantis.
Lights and mirrors create the illusion that this club is bigger than it actually is. The sunken dance floor in the middle of the club is always crowded, and behind the two bars on the perimeter you'll find hot bartenders and top shelf liquor. Tables are reserved for big spenders willing to buy a bottle, and for the uber hot, there's a small private room off the back. This seems to be a popular option for the many celebrities who visit the resort and club, though you'll often find them mingling with the crowd on the dance floor.
The music depends on the crowd and the DJ seems to always know how to find the perfect sounds for each night's audience.

In addition to being a late night gathering place for Atlantis resort guests, Aura has become a favorite nightspot for the local young and hip crowd.

Bimini Road Restaurant

Marina Village, Atlantis Paradise Island. 242-363-3000. www.atlantis. com. See also Must Eat.

Known primarily for its tasty Bahamian fare, Bimini Road is also one of the island's hottest casual nightspots. Each night, a local band sets up on a bandstand and performs Bahamian music and international favorites with a Caribbean twist. There's limited seating at a bar that looks out over the Marina Village, but you can order your cocktail in a 'to go' cup and grab a seat on the wall that lines the marina. It's a great spot for people watching and throughout the evening troupes of dancers stop and put on impromptu shows, teaching

Aura

© Seth Browarnik/Atlantis

visitors of all ages how to move to the Bahamian rhythm.

Cain at the Cove

The Cove, Atlantis, Paradise Island. Open daily from morning til late night. Admission limited.

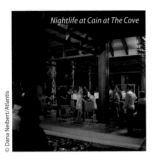

Nightlife at Cain at The Cove

© Dana Neibert/Atlantis

Cain at the Cove is an ultra exclusive adult only pool and beachside club. Situated at the point where Pirate's Cove beach and Paradise Beach meet at a rocky jetty, this is the perfect setting for fun morning, noon and night.
There's a large pool with cushion covered platforms in the middle, multiple bars and even an outdoor casino.
A DJ keeps the place rocking, and with the addition of tiki torches lit at dusk, helps create the ideal night-time club scene as the sun starts to go down.
Part of what makes Cain fabulously cool is that only guests staying at The Cove are allowed in.

Joker's Wild Comedy Club

Between the Beach and Coral Towers, Atlantis, Paradise Island. Doors open 9pm, showtime 9:30pm daily. $20. Adults only.

More plush than your average comedy club, but then, this is Atlantis. Showtime kicks off at 9:30 nightly and is led with house comedian Naughty. He usually pokes fun at some aspect of the Bahamian vacation experience that will have you knowingly laughing out loud even if you've only just arrived on island.
Each night two headlining comedians from the US circuit share the stage.

Junkanoo at Marina Village

Marina Village, Paradise Island. Open Fri & Sat 9:30pm. No Admission fee.

Junkanoo is the quintessential Bahamian celebration of history and culture. It used to be that in order to experience this pulse racing rush of music, costume and dance, you'd need to book your vacation to coincide with one of the two annual Bay Street parades.
Now, every Friday and Saturday night, a troupe of Junkanoo all stars put on their own rush through the meandering walkways of Marina Village.
The minute the drums start beating, the first whistle is blown and the cow bells start their signature 'kalik! kalik!" rhythm, visitors rush out of restaurants and shops to see what's going on.
The costumes are far more simple than the gargantuan crepe paper covered pieces that make their way onto Bay Street, but they are colorful and give you a good idea of what Junkanoo is all about. Feel free to join the group as they make their way through Marina Village, or jump in for a quick photo.

NIGHTLIFE

GRAND BAHAMA ISLAND: FREEPORT & LUCAYA

Referred to as "The Second City," Grand Bahama is developed enough that it's not lumped in with the rest of the Family Islands, but it's never really lived up to the grandiose plans its founders had for it. There is a small city, and quaint settlements from end to end, but much of the 530 square mile island is just waiting for you to explore.

Covered in pines for much of its history, Grand Bahama was first home to Lucayan Indians who inhabited the land prior to the Spanish arrival in the Caribbean. After their decimation, the island supported few inhabitants until the 1870s, when sponge fishermen settled there.

The West End of the island became a major hub for rum runners until the repeal of Prohibition in the United States in the 1930s, and soon thereafter, a blight destroyed Bahamian sponges.

A new boom began in 1944 when the Abaco Lumber Company relocated here, having exhausted the pine forests on Abaco Island. Four years later, Wallace Groves, an American entrepreneur living in the Bahamas, purchased the failing lumber company and turned it around. In 1955, he entered into the Hawksbill Creek Agreement with the government of the Bahamas, paving the way for the creation of a free port on the island.

Under the terms of the agreement, goods could be imported without the heavy duties charged in the rest of the country.

Grand Bahama is the only island that didn't develop 'like topsy' as Bahamians like to say. Instead, the cities of Freeport and Lucaya were meticulously planned; infrastructure for residential and resort areas was laid out around the inland administrative area that was to become Freeport and the oceanside resort area called Lucaya.

The island never quite took off. In

Pelican Point

©Ray Wadia/The Bahamas Ministry of Tourism

an attempt to create the tourism mecca he envisioned, Groves opened a casino at the Lucayan Beach Hotel in 1963. And so it was that gambling, and not commerce, because the lifeblood of the island. Groves' infrastructure was developed to accommodate half a million people, but only about 47,000 people call it home. The network of roads, intended for neighborhoods, lead to dead ends deep in the pine barrens. Activity revolves around resorts and the shopping complexes of Freeport and Lucaya. A recently renovated harbor on the island's southwest edge accommodates a host of cruise and cargo ships.

Straw Weaver, Freeport

©The Bahamas Ministry of Tourism

Freeport

Built as the administrative and commercial core of the island, the 230 square mile city of Freeport revolves around the business and governmental activities of Churchill Square, and what's left of the tourist activities at the International Bazaar. The Royal Oasis resort complex (formerly the Bahamas Princess and Princess Towers), was extensively damaged following back to back hurricanes in 1994 and has never re-opened. Much of the hope for a touristic and economic resurgence in Freeport was pegged to this resort and the city hasn't really rebounded from the blow.

Along the island's west end, a string of small towns are mostly residential, but on the western-most tip, the Old Bahama Bay Resort and a multi-million dollar residential development under construction are creating an exclusive enclave attracting tourists and foreign second home owners.

Lucaya

Lucaya is primarily residential combined with resorts and activities geared towards the island's tourists.

Port Lucaya is the center of activity here, and the hotels of Our Lucaya, a Vegas style casino, dive operations, golf courses and the popular Lucayan Beach make it the most active spot on the entire island. The main attraction of this pretty oceanside resort lies in its proximity to, and accessibility from, America.

While it doesn't have quite the extravagance of **Nassau★**, nor does it have the frenetic atmosphere or sky-high prices.

Heading east, there's a virtually undeveloped 60 mile stretch of island between Lucaya and McLean's town on the eastern tip. Grand Bahama Highway follows the coastline cutting the **Lucayan National Park★★** and through the scrub pine forests that block the ocean view.

Tiny settlements, purely residential, like Free Town, High Rock, Pelican Point, and Rocky Creek are about the only thing to break up the scenery of this isolated area on the way to McLean's Town.

RESORTS

Freeport and Lucaya were designed to attract an upscale client looking for the perfect getaway. Most of the top resorts are within walking distance of the Port Lucaya Marketplace and great Grand Bahama beaches. You will find the most affordable options inland, but most of these lay on free shuttle buses to get you to the beach. For more information and to find hotels not part of major resorts see *Must Stay*.

$$$$$	over $650	$$	$100–$250
$$$$	$400–$650	$	under $100
$$$	$250–$400		

Deep Water Cay Club

$$$$ 9 rooms
Deep Water Cay, off eastern Grand Bahama. 242-353-3077 or 1-912-756-7071. www.deepwatercay.com.

Although the main draw to this resort is bonefishing, the property itself is a far cry from the typical bare bones bonefish lodges found in the islands. Situated on Deep Water Cay, just a few minutes by boat from the tiny settlement of McLean's Town, guests stay in stylishly appointed cottages with porches overlooking the ocean. Despite the remote location, there is plenty to do. There's a pool and lovely private beach. The resort offers bonefishing expeditions to some of the best flats found anywhere. There's a clubhouse where you eat four-course dinners, chat with other guests and use the internet. They also have a small fitness center and spa with two massage rooms.

Old Bahama Bay Resort

$$$ 79 rooms
West End, Grand Bahama. 242-350-6500 or 1-877-949-4466. www.oldbahamabay.com.

You truly are getting away from it all when you stay at this boutique

resort. It's about a 45 minute drive from Freeport and Lucaya, but there's plenty to keep you occupied and all the amenities you'll want or need are right on site. Rooms are luxurious and overlook the ocean or marina. The 2-bedroom suites have huge balconies, perfect for watching the spectacular sunset. Since you're quite a distance from most of the eateries on the island, there is a pool bar serving light snacks, a gourmet restaurant and a more casual one named for "Bonefish Folley Rolle," the Bahamas' best known bonefisherman who lives just up the road.

Pelican Bay at Lucaya

$$ 183 rooms
Seahorse Road at Port Lucaya. 242-373-9550 or 1-800-600-9192. www.pelicanbayhotel.com.

This small resort is a stunning blend of Bahamian and European design. It overlooks Bell Channel Bay, so you can sit on your private balcony watching boats come and go.
Rooms and suites are housed in Danish-style three-story villas and are spacious and elegantly furnished. Wi-Fi is available throughout the property for an added cost.

Pelican Bay at Lucaya

The miles-long Lucaya Beach is just a few minutes' walk away, but there are three pools on property. You're just steps away from the restaurants and bars at bustling Port Lucaya Marketplace, but if you don't feel like venturing out, a new poolside restaurant and bar serves breakfast, lunch and dinner and is open until midnight. Continental breakfast by the pool is included.

Westin and Sheraton Grand Bahama Resort at Our Lucaya

$$ 1,230 rooms
Sea Horse Lane, Lucaya.
242-373-1333 or 1-877-687-5822.
www.ourlucaya.com.

The largest resort property on the island is actually two hotels—a Sheraton and a Westin—on 372 acres right on the beautiful Lucaya Beach.

There's a 38,000 square foot Vegas-style casino, multiple pools, 11 restaurants to satisfy every craving, a spa, tennis, golf, watersports and an award winning kids program. If that's not enough, right across the street is Port Lucaya Marketplace. The hotels—one of them shaped like a cruise ship—have a very art deco feel outside, but step inside for Caribbean elegance.

If the beach is your thing, consider staying here. It's the only property right on Lucaya Beach, offering great views from most rooms.

Viva Wyndham Fortuna Beach

$$ 276 rooms

Churchill Drive & Doubloon Road, Freeport. 242-373-4000 or 1-800-996-3426. www.vivaresorts.com.

Grand Bahama's only all-inclusive resort is great for families. The Kids Club plans indoor and outdoor age appropriate activities for kids

Central pool at The Westin Grand Bahama Island Our Lucaya

RESORTS

81

age 4–12 and is included in the rate so Mom and Dad can enjoy their days in peace and quiet. The large freshwater pool overlooks the ocean and the private beach is hundreds of feet deep. Club Fortuna includes some fun activities from yoga and meditation lessons to local cooking, cocktail classes and make-up application lessons.

Best Western Castaways

$ 118 rooms
East Mall Drive, Freeport.
242-352-6682 or 1-800-937-8376.
www.castaways-resort.com.

This is one of the nicest options at the moment in the Freeport city area. Rooms open up to an exposed balcony in the four-story motel style buildings. Decor is simple tropical, and rooms do have balconies, though the view is nothing to write home about. The resort is right next to the International Bazaar, and a free shuttle will get you to the beach. A full sized pool with bar and a playground for kids provide a pleasant outdoor experience despite the location. Guests have access to a small fitness center and business facility off the lobby.

Ocean Reef Yacht Club & Resort

$ 64 rooms
Bahamas Reef Boulevard.
242-373-4662. www.oryc.com.

A 55-slip marina makes this place popular with the boating crowd. Guests stay in 1, 2 or 3-bedroom townhouses or in 1 or 2-bedroom suites, all fitted with Jacuzzi tubs.

Ocean Reef Yacht Club & Resort

©Ocean Reef Yacht Club & Resort

Rooms have a definite island tropical feel with white tile floors and white rattan furnishings. There are two pools, one with a swim up bar, and a tennis court for guests to use. The onsite restaurant serves Bahamian fare for breakfast, lunch and dinner.

Port Lucaya Resort & Yacht Club

$ 160 rooms
Bell Channel Bay Road, Lucaya.
242-373-6618 or 1-800-582-2921.
www.portlucayaresort.com.

This is a great way to be in the middle of all the action without the hefty price tag of some other resorts in the area. It's right next door to Port Lucaya Marketplace and across the street from the Lucaya Beach. First floor rooms overlook the manicured gardens and Olympic-size swimming pool that's at the center of the resort. Upstairs rooms have balconies overlooking the resort's marina and Bell Channel Bay.
All rooms are a good size, but basic with tile floors, rattan furniture and tropical bedspreads.

CASINOS

When Wallace Groves devised his plan for Grand Bahama, gaming was to be a major feature. Since the 1960s when the cities of Freeport and Lucaya were first developed, there has been casino gambling on the island. In fact, the country's first major casino opened in the old Lucayan Beach Resort in 1964.

Isle of Capri Casino

Our Lucaya, Lucaya.
242-350-2000 or 1-888-687-4753.
www.isleofcapricasino.com/lucaya.

Since hurricanes forced the closure of the Royal Oasis resort in Freeport, the Isle of Capri Casino at Our Lucaya has been the only game in town.

Located between the Sheraton and the Westin, this is the Isle of Capri's only international casino. Try your luck on one of the 323 slots and video poker machines. You can bet anything from a penny to $5. If you want higher stakes, there's a high limit area. The 38,000 square foot glitzy casino also includes 25 tables where you can play craps, blackjack, Caribbean stud, mini baccarat, roulette and three card poker. High rollers will like the private Jewel of the Isle, featuring high limit tables, a sports book and race book.

At the Cove Bar within the casino, you can catch all the hot games on TV.

The Isle of Capri Casino is open from 10am–5am, but slot machines go full throttle around the clock on weekends.

The casino hosts special tournaments and events throughout the year.

You must be 18 or over to gamble in the casino, and Bahamian citizens and residents are prohibited from gambling by law.

© Our Lucaya Resort

Isle of Capri Casino

BEACHES

What Grand Bahama lacks when it comes to centuries-old history in much of the rest of the Bahamas and the always on vibe found in **Nassau★**, it makes up for in beaches. 96 miles from end to end, the fourth largest island in the chain is lined with miles-long unspoiled beaches that go days and weeks without a human being on them.

Fortune Beach★

*East of Taino Beach,
Grand Bahama.*

This is a true treasure worth seeking. It's long and usually very quiet even though there is a small restaurant and bar there. The beach got its name for a $2 million dollar shipwreck discovered offshore.

Taino Beach★

Jolly Roger Drive, Lucaya.

Taino Beach is generally quiet during the week, coming to life on the weekends when locals flock here for the various activities hosted by the bars and restaurants situated here. The Stoned Crab, Kaptain Kenny's and Toni Macaroni's are all great places to grab lunch or dinner after a day of swimming and sunning.

A small playground area and shallow, sandy-bottomed waters makes this a perfect spot to bring young children.

Taino Beach itself is picture postcard perfect—long and deep with talcum power white sand. You won't find much in the way of watersports here, but occasionally a lady will stroll along asking if you want your hair braided.

On Wednesday night's the area comes alive at nearby Smith's Point, home of the highly popular fish fry.

Coral Beach

Royal Palm Way, Lucaya.

Just west of the busy Lucayan Beach, you'll find Coral Beach. It's just as lovely, but since it's quite a walk away from the resorts, not many visitors bother to make the

Gold Rock Beach

Xanadu Beach

trek. Grab your towel and sunblock and stroll or power walk your way into peace and quiet. If you get hungry, head to Billy Joe's snack shack for some roast conch.

Gold Rock Beach

Grand Bahama Highway, Grand Bahama.

Part of this beautiful beach is included in the **Lucayan National Park★★**. 12 miles away from Lucaya, you'll probably put the first footprints of the day on this beach no matter what time you get there. Weekends and holidays it's a popular picnic spot for locals and their families.

Lucayan Beach

Royal Palm Way, Lucaya.

This miles-long stretch has long been one of the island's busiest beaches. The Our Lucaya Resort is right on it, and all the other resorts in the area claim it as their own. This is your best bet if you're looking for watersports. Jet ski, banana boat and parasail operators walk the beach, offering their wares.

You can also rent hobie cats and windsurf boards by the hour or the day *(Ocean Motion Water Sports. 242-374-2425).*

Beach volleyball courts belong to the Our Lucaya Resort, but you can generally get in on a game.

There's a host of beach bars lining the beach so you can quench your thirst with a 'daiquiri' or 'Bahama Mama.'

This is the most popular beach in large part because of its proximity to the major tourism hub.

Xanadu Beach

Sunken Treasure Drive, Freeport.

For those staying in Freeport, this is a quick beach to get to. The Xanadu Hotel, where American recluse Howard Hughes occupied two floors before his death, still towers over the beach, but many of the rooms have been closed so it's really never crowded.

A handful of straw vendors will try to convince you to take home a souvenir from their stock and you'll find most watersports along the mile-long beach.

BEACHES

PARKS AND GARDENS

Wallace Groves wasn't focused just on bricks and mortar when it came to developing his dream city. He created the wondrous Garden of the Groves in 1973. Other National Parks have been developed over the years, giving locals and tourists a chance to commune with nature.

Lucayan National Park

©Ray Wadia/The Bahamas Ministry of Tourism

Lucayan National Park★★

Grand Bahama Highway, Grand Bahama. 242-352-5438. Open daily 9–4pm. $3.

The six miles of caves, caverns and tunnels are considered the longest underwater cavern system in the world. It's a diver's dream. But the 40 acre park is fantastic to explore even if you have no intention of getting wet.

Situated about 20 miles east of Freeport, the park, which is managed by the Bahamas National Trust, contains nature trails, an elevated boardwalk and access to two large caves. One of the caves is a prime habitat for migratory bats, which does mean it's closed during their nursing season each summer. You're safe to venture in at other times of the year as bats are rabies-free in the Bahamas.

The other cave is where archaeologists found remains of indigenous Lucayan Indians. As a result, this cave is called Burial Mound. Wander along the wooden boardwalk where you'll see wild bromeliads and orchids. The park also includes part of the Gold Rock Creek and neighboring beach, so it includes the island's five very different ecosystems.

Rand Nature Center★

East Settler's Way, Freeport. 242-352-5438. Open Mon–Fri 9am–4pm. $5.

This 100-acre sanctuary was the first of its kind for the Bahamas and was designed to preserve nature for generations to come.

There are marked nature trails meandering throughout, and signs identifying the more than 130 native plants and in some cases, giving an explanation of their use over the years.

Perhaps the biggest draw is a chance to see West Indian Flamingos up close. Other birds call the Rand Nature Center home, antillean peewees, red-legged thrushes, stripe-headed tanagers, and the endangered Bahama Parrot. There's a small gift shop at the center where you can pick up local art, books and jewelry.

Garden of the Groves

Midshipman Road and Magellan Drive, Freeport. 242-373-5668.

Much tender loving care and a lot of money is returning The Garden of the Groves to its glory days. Once one of the finest botanical gardens in the region, the gardens were devastated following the 2004 hurricane season. Left un-attended for three years, the glorious foliage died, the gardens became overgrown, structures crumbled and much of the wildlife left for greener pastures.

In 2008, the Garden of the Groves was re-opened, although work to completely transform it continues on a daily basis.

The 12 acres contain specimens of more than 10,000 species of exotic trees, plants and flowers from all over the world. Throughout there are cascading waterfalls and ponds alive with fish and turtles. The decision was made recently to find a more appropriate home for the alligator that had taken up residence.

The focal point remains the chapel on the hill. This stone covered single room chapel with wooden benches and a bell tower has been painstakingly restored and consecrated, making it once again a favorite place for weddings, christenings and simple reflection.

A new feature has been added to the peaceful oasis. The labyrinth is an exact replica of the famous labyrinth at Chartres Cathedral near Paris, France. Walk the sacred path to renewal and transformation. Make a day of it and grab a light lunch at the new *Lofty Fig Cafe* with its three-tiered outdoor terrace.

Garden of the Groves

PARKS AND GARDENS

NATURAL SITES

On Grand Bahama you will find that many of the natural sites are part of official National Parks and centers, and this is testament to the Government's drive to cultivate eco tourism. However, there are still beautiful natural sites to discover off the tourist trail.

Gold Rock Creek

©Ray Wadia/The Bahamas Ministry of Tourism

Gold Rock Creek

Grand Bahama Highway.
Closed to the public.

In 2005, Grand Bahama was awash with swashbuckling pirates once again. Significant portions of Pirates of the Caribbean I and II were filmed at the Gold Rock Creek Studios. The unique $10 million water tank was a huge draw for the producers. Since then, the film studio has been abandoned and is in the midst of a long, drawn out sale process. Plans initially called for the development of a resort hotel, water park, theme restaurants, bars, merchandising outlets and tourist attractions, but so far, nothing has come of it.

Smiling Pat's Adventures

Freeport native Smiling Pat (yes, that is how she introduces herself) has some unique tours that combine culture and nature. Head into Pelican Point and interact with some of the wise old souls who've seen this place change over the years. You'll find out about the history of sponging, learn how to plait straw and get a demo on everything coconut—from climbing the tree to cooking with the delicacy. The West End tour visits Smiling Pat's grandmother's bakery for some of the best native treats to satisfy a sweet tooth. From there you'll venture along the heritage trail to the Hermitage and also visit an old church as well as the remains of the island's first hotel. Another tour takes you to Lightbourn's Cay just off McLean's Town. This uninhabited 8-mile long sandy island was the setting for an episode of The Bachelor. Here, you'll learn how to hand line fish the way the locals do. Whatever you catch is what's for dinner. *Freeport, Grand Bahama. 242-533-2946, 242-533-3335 or 242-727-0006. www.smilingpat.com.*

GRAND BAHAMA ISLAND

MUST SEE

The water tank, adjacent marina, 250,000 square foot staging area, and film related buildings aren't much to look at and you can't get inside, but it's cool to say you and Captain Jack (Johnny Depp's character) were in the same place, albeit at different times.

Before the film studio set up shop, Gold Rock Creek was home to a long time decommissioned 3,500-acre US Air Force missile-tracking station that was built in 1951.

HISTORIC SITES

Once the Spanish had decimated the Lucayan population, apart from pirates who exploited the treacherous reef, the island was largely ignored for 400 years. The American Civil War and Prohibition brought short lived prosperity to the island as it became a hub for smuggling to the USA. The **Lucayan National Park★★** *(see p 86)* is a great place to learn about the original inhabitants of Grand Bahama; there are few other historic sites as nothing was here for so long.

The Hermitage

Freetown, Grand Bahama.

All that remains of this island's oldest known building is a stone shell. But exploring something that dates back to 1901 on an island where most things didn't arrive until the 1950s is exciting.

The Hermitage is believed to have once housed slaves. In fact, Freetown is the first place slaves were freed following emancipation in the 1830s.

The ruins lie along what is called **The Heritage Trail** *(see p 92)*, which is a five-mile nature trail. Phone *Grand Bahama Nature Tours* (242-373-2485) to arrange a guided visit, or you can explore on your own.

Ye Olde Pirate Bottle House

Port Lucaya Marketplace, Lucaya. 242-373-2000. Open 9am–5pm. $3.

This rather large private collection of antique bottles is worth a look. Some date back to the 1600s, others have a younger vintage. The displays explain the significance of each bottle, providing a time line as well as a likely use. There's everything from gin bottles to ink wells and the notorious poison vessel. The display also explains why different bottles have different shapes and are made of different types of glass.

Smith's Point Fish Fry

A series of shacks set up overlooking the water, Smith's Point Fish Fry is down home simplicity at its best. **Wednesday nights**, it seems the entire population plus all the tourists on island head to 'the fry' to dance to live music on sandy dance floors, catch up on the latest gossip, and eat some of the best fried snapper and conch fritters ever made. *Smith's Point, east of Lucaya.*

SHOPPING

You're not going to find as much in the way of designer shopping here as you will in **Nassau★**, but it's a far better selection than on most of the other islands. The two main shopping centers are the dated International Bazaar and the whimsical Port Lucaya Marketplace.

🐚 Port Lucaya

Sea Horse Drive, Lucaya. 242-373-8446. www.portlucayamarketplace.com.

Port Lucaya Marketplace

© Bahamas Tourist Office

This open air festival-style marketplace is the heartbeat of Grand Bahama's prime tourism arena. Eighty shops, housed in pastel buildings offer an impressive selection of items. You can find anything from locally made crafts to high end designer products. Many items are duty free here so expect good deals on things like perfume, cosmetics and designer bags. Pop into **Flovin's Gallery** and **Leos Art Gallery** for some unique pieces of art as well as some higher end local craft goods. There's also a **Straw Market** at Port Lucaya. It's the only place on the island where you can bargain for goods. Try to get the vendor down about 15–20 percent of the asking price. Most of the straw work is imported, although a few vendors do sell locally crafted items. This is a good spot to pick up t-shirts and souvenirs. Most stores are open 10am–6pm and the straw vendors will stay open a bit later if they sense an opportunity to make a sale.

Wood carvings on sale at Straw Market, Freeport

©Ray Wadia/The Bahamas Ministry of Tourism

GRAND BAHAMA ISLAND

MUST DO

International Bazaar

West Sunrise Highway and East Mall Drive. 242-352-2828.

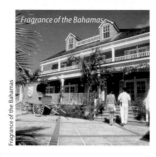

Fragrance of the Bahamas

Fragrance of the Bahamas

The world famous Japanese Torii gates still welcome you to this landmark shopping center, but following the devastating 2004 hurricane season and the subsequent closure of the Royal Oasis resort next door, The International Bazaar has sunk further and further into disrepair.

That said, it's still worth wandering through the corridors that lead you from one part of the world into another. Many of the shops have struggled to remain open, but a few have stood the test of time and offer deals and goods not found elsewhere. The **Glass Blower Shop** *(242-352-8585)* has been around for decades. Artist Sidney Pratt still entertains the crowds with his hand blown techniques. Pick up one of his delicate signature island-inspired pieces or order a custom souvenir.

The **Bahamas Coin & Stamp** store *(242-352-8989)* has been around for decades as well. It's tiny but has a pretty impressive selection of coins and stamps from around the world. True collectors and those just looking for something different to take home can check here for first day issues of Bahamian stamps from years gone by and mint condition Bahamian coins. Try to get a 15¢ coin. It hasn't been in circulation for many years, but this round edged square coin is a neat find.

Create your own fragrance at **Fragrance of the Bahamas** Limited (The Perfume Factory). *(242-352-9391, www.perfume factory.com.)* It's housed in a colonial style building in the rear of the International Bazaar. Take a factory tour and learn how their signature scents are created. Each bottle of Sand Cologne has a bit of Bahamian sand inside, and the bottles of Pink Pearl contain a conch shell pearl.

Havana Trading Company

Across from Isle of Capri Casino, Our Lucaya, Lucaya. 242-351-5685.

If you're in the market for some authentic Cuban stogies to smoke while on vacation, this is the best place to avoid getting fakes. They have a vast selection in the large walk-in humidor and there are Cuban cigar rollers working on the premises.

Sun & Sea Outfitters

UNEXSO, Lucaya. 242-373-1244.

In order to truly take advantage of all the water based activities Grand Bahama has to offer, chances are you're going to need to pick up some gear. They have everything from bathing suits and sunglasses to cameras and snorkeling gear.

SHOPPING

NATURE TOURS

There is so much to see and do in Grand Bahama so long as you pack your sense of adventure along with your bathing suit. From swimming with wild dolphins to exploring bat caves to meeting friendly natives eager to share history and culture, there's a tour for every interest.

Grand Bahama Nature Tours

Freeport, Grand Bahama. 242-373-2485 or 1-866-440-4542.www. grandbahamanaturetours.com.

The folks at Grand Bahama Nature Tours (formerly Kayak Nature Tours) have mastered the art of getting off the beaten path.
Whether you opt for a 20-mile bicycle tour of nearby settlements and the dolphins at Sanctuary Bay, kayaking through mangroves in the **Lucayan National Park★★** followed by a guided nature walk and visits of the caves, or a guided jeep safari that takes you off road to places you'd never otherwise see, you're in for an informative and memorable experience. Grand Bahama Nature Tours has been in operation for more than 15 years and all the guides are naturalists who've taken the

Bahamahost program. Depending on your tour, you'll have a certified lifeguard and experienced kayak and snorkel instructor and guide. All tours include transportation to and from all Freeport and Lucaya hotels as well as lunch and refreshments.

The Heritage Trail

Old Freetown to Eight Mile Rock.

This undemanding 5-mile trek is a great way to get in touch with nature on Grand Bahama Island. The dirt road running from east to west was once the island's main road, but since the development of the modern highway, has been reclaimed by nature. Along the way there are over 30 types of plant, 18 kinds of birds and an array of dazzling butterflies. You will also come across the ruins of The Hermitage *(see p 89)*.

Kayaking in Grand Bahama

© The Bahamas Ministry of Tourism

OUTDOOR SPORTS

Grand Bahama has all the outdoor activities you'd expect of a large resort destination. There are three championship golf courses, most large hotels have tennis and you can ride horses on the beach.

Reef Course at Sunset

©Our Lucaya Resort

Golf

Fortune Hills Golf and Country Club

East Sunrise Highway, Lucaya. 242-373-4500. $53 for 9 holes, $70 for 18 holes. Includes cart rental.

Not as challenging as the other two courses on the island, this course was designed by Dick Wilson and Joe Lee in 1971. Although it only has 9 physical holes, different tee placements create distinctively different shots for 18 holes.

Lucayan Golf Course

The Westin and Sheraton Grand Bahama Island Resort. 242-373-2002. Resort guests $120, non guests $140. Includes cart rental.

This 6,824 yard course was designed by Dick Wilson and has been challenging golfers since 1962. It's par 72 with 18 holes. Tif dwarf grass gives you a superior putting surface.

Reef Course

The Westin and Sheraton Grand Bahama Island Resort Reef Course. 242-373-2002. Resort guests $120, non guests $140. Includes cart rental.

Thirteen of the 18 holes on this 6,930 yard course, designed by Robert Trent Jones Jr. feature beautiful lakes. This unique links-style course has large, winding fairways and gently rolling hills.

Tennis

Westin at Our Lucaya. 242-373-1333.

While most hotels have courts, The Westin at Our Lucaya takes tennis to another level. They've got all four surfaces covered—the hard court featuring Decoturf, the Rebound Ace court, the impeccably

93

manicured English grass court and a French red brick clay court.

Horseback Riding

Pinetree Stables, Beachway Drive, Freeport. 242-373-3600. www.pinetree-stables.com. $85 for 2hrs.

Twice daily trail rides leave the stables and head through the pine forests past a castle, over sand dunes and onto a secluded beach where you and your horse can trot along and take a swim. The minimum age is 8, weight limit is 200 pounds and you don't have to have any riding experience.

WATERSPORTS

On most beaches you'll find banana boat rides, waterskiing and parasailing. However, this large island is surrounded by amazing coral reefs, so it should come as no surprise that there are some impressive dive and snorkel sites. More experienced divers will find exploring the world's longest underwater cavern system a thrilling experience. There are dolphin and shark dives, too.

Dive Sites

Ben's Cavern

Named for the Grand Bahama native who discovered this natural marvel, Ben's Cavern is part of the extensive **Lucayan National Park★★**. It's part of the world's longest known underwater cavern system. The perfect place to get your feet wet with cave diving, you can go down 50ft into the cavern without ever losing sight of the large opening.

You'll swim through stalactites and stalagmites as you venture from the cool freshwater cavern pool into the warmer saltwater deeper in. This cave is closed from late spring into early summer to allow the bats that live here to nurse their young.

Admiring the reefs

©The Bahamas Ministry of Tourism

Gold Rock (Ben's) Blue Hole

The horse show shaped ledge of this blue hole has interesting marine life to start you off. Total depths go to about 50ft, there's good visibility and a gentle current. Coral heads teem with jacks, snapper, and other beautiful fish.

The Jose

This steel hulled vessel was deliberately sunk in 1986. The 45 foot long, 20 foot wide work boat had been abandoned at the rear of a derelict hotel. When the hotel was about to re-open, the new owners arranged to have the eyesore sunk offshore. It lies in about 65ft of water and is a good first dive.

Papa Doc's Wreck

Named for Haiti's former ruthless leader, this is actually the wreck of a 70 foot boat used by mercenaries headed to fight in the revolution against Papa Doc Duvalier. They never made it, their boat sank in about 45ft of water during a storm in 1968. Fish teem around this relatively shallow wreck.

Peterson's Cay National Park

Peterson's Cay, is the Bahamas' smallest protected national park. The island is just 1½ acres, but the surrounding ¼ mile of marine habitat is also protected by the Bahamas National Trust.
The shallow sand bars and rich reefs are ideal for snorkeling or scuba diving. You can get there by boat or by kayak, but be sure to anchor in a sandy spot so as not to damage any of the reefs. Parrot fish and dolphin are common sights and there's a myriad of corals and

sea fans, including the painful fire coral, so don't touch.

Sea Star II Wreck

This 180 foot long ship was laid to rest on the ocean floor in 2002. She sits upright in about 90ft of water and has a cavernous cargo hold that's great for exploring. The wreck is now home to a large variety of fish and has some of the biggest arrow crabs you'll find. On the deck is a small crane and experienced divers may want to check out the galley, crew quarters and wheelhouse.

Shark Alley

As many as 20 Caribbean reef sharks come out to greet divers each day at this sandy spot. You'll be about 45ft below the surface while qualified professionals protected by a special mesh steel suit, feed the sharks.

SPID City

Home to a SPID—Self Contained Portable Inflatable Dwelling—used in habitation experiments in the 1970s. This 60 foot dive is also where you'll find a twin engine Aztec aircraft used in the "Sea Hunt" series. This sandy bottom dive is teeming with beautiful parrot fish and the occasional shark.

Theo's Wreck

This 1954 ship, the MS Logna, was decommissioned and then abandoned at the Grand Bahama cement company dock in the early-1980s. Rather than scuttle it in the deep ocean, a dive enthusiast, Theo Galanopulos, made a convincing argument to have it go down in shallow waters, thus creating one of the island's most

95

spectacular wreck dives.

It now lies about 1½ miles offshore about 100ft below the surface. The wreck is about 230ft long and rests between a reef and the ocean drop off.

Sharks, rays, turtles, grunts and lobster have made a home here.

Treasure Reef

Don't go here expecting to strike it rich. In the mid-1960s, four young locals discovered this old Spanish wreck and several thousand silver coins worth about $3 million. But it's a safe bet all the treasure's been unearthed since then. Today, you'll find a rich sealife including multicolored French grunts, sea fans, brain coral and majestic elkhorn corals.

The Dolphin Experience

Underwater Explorers Society (UNEXSO), Lucaya. 242-373-1244 or 1-800-992-3483. www.unexso.com.

One of the first dolphin interaction programs in the country, it remains one of the most popular.

Diving with Dolphins

UNEXSO was the first scuba operator to offer dolphin encounters and there's no better way to observe these amazing creatures in their natural habitat than by donning a scuba tank and diving alongside the pods. UNEXSO offer this unique experience as well as discover scuba diving courses for beginners and a range of other dive experiences.

UNEXSO's 14 resident dolphins actually live at a 9-acre Dolphin Experience Lagoon in Sanctuary Bay, about a 2-mile ferry ride away. You'll learn all about these fascinating mammals regardless of which program you opt for.

The **Dolphin Close Encounter** is ideal for younger children and anyone not quite ready to take the plunge. You'll get to interact with dolphins from a floating dock and then go on a waist deep-submerged platform to touch one. (Adults $75, children 4–7 $50, children under 4 free.)

You'll get in the lagoon with the

Swimming with a dolphin at the Dolphin Experience

© The Bahamas Ministry of Tourism

dolphins and learn how to get them to leap and twirl at your command in the **Swim with Dolphins** program. (Minimum height 55", $169.)

For the ultimate encounter, sign up for the **Open Ocean Experience** where you and a group of these trained wild Atlantic Bottle-nose Dolphins will venture out to sea for a half hour of playtime. (Minimum height 55", $199.)

It's a good idea to book ahead of time as the programs tend to fill up fast.

Snorkeling

Most resorts rent out snorkel gear so that you can snorkel just off the beach, however for the most picturesque spots it is definitely worth booking a tour. Several reputable companies organize popular trips that you can book through your hotel.

Fantasia Tours

242-373-8681. www.snorkeling bahamas.com. Departs daily 10.30am, 2.10am. $40, children $20.

Pat and Diane offer far more than a routine snorkel excursion. Their half day sea safari goes out on a 72-foot catamaran outfitted with a water slide and rock climbing wall. You'll cruise through the Lucayan canal to a shallow reef, ideal for safe snorkeling. Be sure to buy a bag of fish food to take in with you. All equipment is provided.

©The Bahamas: Ministry of Tourism

Snorkeling in Freeport

Grand Bahama Nature Tours

Pick up from hotels in the Freeport and Lucaya area starts from 9am. See p 92 for contact information. $79.

See p 92 for contact information.

This well-loved eco-tour operator organizes snorkel tours to **Peterson's Cay National Park** *(see Dive Sites)*. In the air conditioned mini-vans on the way, friendly guides will chat about the history, flora and fauna of the island. You are given basic paddling and safety instruction and it takes about 30 minutes to kayak across to the Cay. Snorkeling is just off the beach and all equipment, including waterproof bags for valuables, is included in the price. You'll be snorkeling for about and hour and a half, and the entire trip takes about 5 hours.

WATERSPORTS

97

NIGHTLIFE

From sandy bars to Bahamian shows to high energy discos, Grand Bahama's nightlife runs the gamut. Be sure to check with your hotel or call ahead to make sure a place is open as many have cut back with slower tourist seasons lately.

Bahama Mama Sunset Cruise and Show

Freeport. 242-373-7863. www.superiorwatersports.com. Dinner cruise $79; booze cruise $45.

Surf n Turf dinner, unlimited refills of wine or the potent Bahama Mama punch, live native entertainment and spectacular sunsets—it just doesn't get better than this. The 72 foot Bahama Mama cata-maran sets sail nightly just before sunset and sails the waters around Freeport and Lucaya for 2–3 hours. After dinner, the music gets going and everyone hits the dance floor.

Club Amnesia

East Mall Drive, Freeport. 242-351-2582. Opening nights vary by season. Cover charge ranges from $10–$20.

This is the island's most quintessential nightclub. Huge mirrors, strobe lights and gaudy colors set the scene inside. The club opens at 9:30, but there's really no point in going much before midnight. Don't worry, you'll still get a full night of partying as the club doesn't close until you've had enough. The crowd is mainly young locals.

> **Local Brew**
>
> Sands beer has only been on the market a year but it's gained such popularity with locals and tourists all over the Bahamas that they have a hard time keeping up with demand. The brewery is planning on offering tours and has a few more brews in the pipeline.

Limbo Dancing

©The Bahamas Ministry of Tourism

The Prop Club at the Sheraton Grand Bahama Island Our Lucaya

© Our Lucaya Resort

Count Basie Square

*Port Lucaya Marketplace, Lucaya.
Thu–Sat nights.*

After dinner, stroll over to Count
Basie Square, a large, open air
area with a stage that gets going
around 8pm. You can dance, sway,
sit, or sip a tropical drink at one of
the four popular bars rimming the
square. Entertainment ranges from
calypso to reggae to R&B. Most
nights the limbo dancers come
out to thrill the crowd with their
incredible flexibility.
The square was named after the
renowned jazz band leader who
used to have a home on the island.

Native Slice at
Club Amnesia

*East Mall Drive, Freeport.
242-351-2582, or 242-352-3587.
Mon, Wed and Fri.*

Dinner and a show is a hard
combination to come by on the
island these days. Club Amnesia
fills the void with an action packed
native show complete with limbo
dancers, fire dancing, steel pan
band and lots more to wow you.

Shenanigans

*Port Lucaya Marketplace, Lucaya.
242-373-4734.*

Pay homage to the Bahamas' colonial past and have the bartender
pour you a mug of draft Guinness.
Get a good, hearty meal here at
the island's only Irish pub before
you start your night of partying.

The Prop Club Sports
Bar & Dance Club

*Westin and Sheraton Grand
Bahama Island Resort.
242-373-1333.*

Many nights, the party at this place
spills out outside, over the patio
and onto the sand.
There's a huge dance floor inside,
and live music most nights to
get and keep the party going all
night long. Some nights you can
take the stage with the karaoke
machine and on Sundays, sports
takes over on big screen televisions. Depending on the season
management hosts various theme
nights from Junkanoo to games.

ANDROS, BERRY AND BIMINI ISLANDS

The northwestern-most islands of the Bahamian archipelago are a playground for those seeking plentiful fishing, spectacular diving and phenomenal natural sites. Although there are regulars who return year after year, you're not going to be just one of the crowd here.

ANDROS

By far the largest of all the Bahamian islands at 104mi-long and 40mi-wide, Andros is also the most sparsely populated.

The "Big Yard," or "Sleeping Giant" as locals call it, offers some of the most incredible pristine and remote sites for the avid ecotourist. With miles and miles of untouched beaches, you will spend days beach combing and never see another soul.

Just off the coast of Andros lies the second-largest **barrier reef★★★** in the northern hemisphere; the third largest in the world. Just a bit further off the coast lies the **Tongue of the Ocean** *(see p 108)* a 6,000ft deep tongue-shaped area of water that can be seen from space. Inland, the landscape is dotted with hundreds of blue holes (also known as sinkholes, or vertical caves). With such a variety of sites, Andros has long been a favorite destination for scuba divers.

Creatures of All Kinds

With so much land, Andros is home to a wide variety of wildlife. Flamingos hang out on the west coast, rarely disturbed by humans. A protected National Park contains one of the largest populations of white-crowned pigeon found anywhere in the world. Wild boar and land crabs have the run of the land.

You probably won't get to see one of Andros' most infamous creatures—the mythical chickcharnie. Said to live deep in the pine forests, these half-human, half-bird, elfin-like critters hang from tree branches by their tails.

If you do stumble across a chickcharnie, be careful: They're said to

Aerial view of Andros

Blue Hole, Nicholl's Town, Andros

©The Bahamas Ministry of Tourism

The Berry Islands have beautiful beaches, many a boat ride away on uninhabited cays, as well as incredible dive sites and great fishing.

THE BIMINI ISLANDS

The islands that make up Bimini span 28 miles, and are the westernmost islands in the entire chain of Bahama islands.

Lying just 50 miles off the coast of Florida, Bimini has a colorful and romantic past—pirates are said to have plundered merchant ships crossing the Atlantic and buried their treasure on the island, and in the days of prohibition in the United States, rum runners stored their bootleg here. Myths and legends cling to these islands, not least that this is the place where the lost continent of Atlantis lies, or the location of the mythical Fountain of Youth.

Renowned author Ernest Hemingway helped put Bimini on the map when he wrote about his favorite Bahama getaway in *Islands in the Stream*.

Deep waters teeming with gamefish have since helped earn these islands the title "Big Game Fishing Capital of the World" and attracts visitors in the summer, usually considered the Bahamas' low season.

It is also a popular destination for the wealthy yachting set. Interested in diving? One of the most popular diving sites near the island is the wreck of the Sapona. In the 1920s it was used to run liquor between Bimini and Florida and was used as a speakeasy while docked at the island. The infamous boat hit a reef and sank during the 1929 hurricane.

have mystical powers and will turn your head backwards if you have bad thoughts.

Treasure Hunting

Like much of the Bahamas, Andros was once inhabited by pirates. Morgan's Bluff, one of the island's northernmost settlements, is named for the dastardly pirate Henry Morgan, who once called the area home. It's said that he buried his treasure here for safekeeping; no one's ever been able to find it and prove the tale true.

THE BERRY ISLANDS

The small islands north of Andros have always been a playground for the rich and famous. In its heyday, old Hollywood frequented "The Berries," as locals often refer to the group of tiny islands.

Today, exclusive enclaves are tucked away on many of the 30 cays that make up the Berry Islands.

Most of the 600 year-round residents live on Great Harbour Cay, which is just 6mi-long by 2½mi-wide.

RESORTS AND SPAS

Don't head to Andros, Berry or Bimini looking for glitzy megaresorts: Accommodations here are more simple, though some resorts have managed to put an upscale twist on island living. For more information and to find hotels not part of major resorts, see *Must Stay*.

$$$$$	over $650	$$	$100–$250
$$$$	$400–$650	$	under $100
$$$	$250–$400		

RESORTS

⚓ Kamalame Cay

$$$$$ 23 rooms
Kamalame Cay, Staniard Cay, Andros. 242-368-6281 or 1-800-790-7971. www.kamalame.com.

Accessible only by private ferry or seaplane, exclusive Kamalame Cay is situated on a 96-acre private island across a narrow channel from Andros. The villas and cottages are laid out in a manner which provides absolute privacy for guests. The colonial-style rooms are designed to take advantage of all the cay has to offer; they feature 20-foot high ceilings and huge French windows
From the elegant Indonesian furnishings and oversized soaking tubs and showers with ocean views to fresh-baked cookies left in your room each afternoon, no detail is left to chance.
Rates include all top-shelf liquor and meals—candlelit dinners, restaurant or boxed lunches to take on a day's adventure, and breakfast made to order.
The island has a three-mile long stretch of powdery white sand as well as a heated swimming pool.

Little Whale Cay Resort

$$$$$ 3 villas
Little Whale Cay, The Berry Islands. 242 326 9216. www.littlewhale cay.com.

This stunning private island retreat can be hired out in its entirety, accommodating up to 12 guests in three luxury villas. The island is fully staffed with a 13-strong team, including a masseur, tennis pro, bonefish guide, and personal

Kamalame Cay

chef. In addition to its infinity pool overlooking the sea, there's a gym, tennis court, private airstrip, harbor and flotilla of boats that can be used for fishing, cruising or watersports; in fact there is everything here that you could want—and most of all, privacy.

Andros Island Bonefish Club

$$$$ 12 rooms
*Cargill Creek, Andros.
242-368-5167. www.androsbone
fishing.com.*

Andros is the bonefishing capital of the world and this tiny lodge has done a great job of catering to this niche market since 1984. AIBC is owned and operated by one of the country's top bonefishing guides, Rupert Leadon. Rooms are simple, but spacious enough for all your fishing gear. Bedrooms overlook the flats you'll spend the day on. There's a small pool, fully stocked bar and family-style dining room on site. Rates include meals, bottled water, guided fishing and boat trips, taxes, and laundry service.

Bimini Bay Resort and Marina

$$$ 334 rooms
*North Bimini. 242-347-2900.
www.biminibayresort.com.*

Occupying its own peninsula with the Atlantic Ocean on one side and the tranquil Bimini Bay on the other, Bimini Bay Resort offers stunning water views at every turn. Accommodations range from the spacious single-bedroom suites to the sprawling four-bedroom water-front homes that comfortably sleep up to ten people.
All are located in Caribbean-style pastel-colored villas situated in a way that gives the resort a neighborhood feel. Rooms are outfitted with all the amenities to make a longer stay comfortable, including kitchenettes and kitchens, laundry facilities, televisions and internet connection. There are a number of beaches, as well as a luxurious pool overlooking the ocean. Bimini Bay goes the extra mile to cater to children. Young guests can spend their time in the 2,100-square foot children's facility, where there are video games and plenty of activities to keep them occupied.

Andros Bonefishing Club

Tiamo Resorts bathroom

©Joe Blackburn/Progressive Earth Development

Small Hope Bay Lodge

$$$ 21 rooms
Fresh Creek, Andros. 242-368-2014 or 1-800-223-6961. www. smallhope.com.

Rustic but comfortable, Small Hope Bay is the perfect place to get away from it all. Outside of the office, there are no phones, no televisions, no Wi-Fi to distract you from doing nothing and enjoying the peace and quiet.
Rooms are constructed of coral rock and native Andros Pine beams, and only some of them have air conditioning, so be sure to make your needs known at booking if this is a must.
The one- and two-bedroom cottages are located right on the beach and have magnificent ocean views.
Small Hope Bay is a favorite with scuba divers and has a fully equipped dive shop on site.
Rates include food and drinks, free Discover Scuba or refresher lessons, non-motorized watersports equipment and bicycle rental.

🐚 Tiamo Resorts

$$$ 11 rooms
South Andros Island, Andros. 242-357-2489. www.tiamoresorts.com.

Considered the best example of an eco-resort in the entire Caribbean, Tiamo Resorts sets the standard for luxury living while preserving the environment.
The resort is accessible only by boat, and there are no modern day interruptions like telephones, televisions, internet or even cell phone signal in the guest rooms.
Guests stay in elegantly decorated

Small Hope Bay Lodge

©The Bahamas Ministry of Tourism

single room beachside bungalows with open-air showers, wrap-around porches, hammocks and lounge chairs on the beach.
Let the nature concierge team come up with an adventure for you each day—perhaps one of the daily biologist-guided eco-tours. Tiamo does not permit children under the age of 14. Rates include everything except beverages.

Bimini Big Game Resort and Yacht Club

$$ 47 rooms
Alice Town, Bimini.
242-347-3391 or 1-800-737-1007.
www.biminibiggame.com.

Just 50 miles away from South Florida, the resort and marina are ideally located for boaters looking for a weekend (or longer) getaway. Even if you don't have a boat, this resort is a great spot. Rooms were recently renovated and are located in a motel-style, two-story building. The simple but spacious rooms have a porch or balcony overlooking the marina and swimming pool, and there's Wi-Fi available throughout the resort.

There are two restaurants on site serving mainly Bahamian fare, and the sports bar by the pool is where fishermen gather at the end of the day to compare their catch.

Emerald Palms

$$ 50 rooms
Congo Town, South Andros.
242-369-2713. www.emerald-palms.com.

Whether you opt to spend your vacation in one of the Clubhouse guest rooms with floor-to-ceiling windows overlooking the ocean or in one of the lavishly appointed one- and two-bedroom villas, you're in for a treat.
Marble floors, rich mahogany doors, king size beds and Jacuzzi bathtubs are only the start of this colonial style elegance.
If you tire of lounging pool side, arrange an adventure through the concierge. Rent a bicycle and explore the neighborhood, kayak through the mangroves or take a guided hike through the bushes to visit blue holes and learn about local bush medicine.

Bimini Big Game Resort and Yacht Club

©The Bahamas Ministry of Tourism

RESORTS AND SPAS

Emerald Palms

©The Bahamas Ministry of Tourism

Chub Cay Club Resort & Marina

$ 24 rooms
Chub Cay, Berry Islands.
242-325-1490. www.chubcay.com.

For more than 40 years, this small resort has been a favorite, exclusive club-style home away from home. A few years ago, a group of American investors took it over, completely overhauled it and turned it into a true gem.
There's still a membership program that offers reduced rates for villa and marina slip rental, but non-members are always welcome.
Guest villas are brand new, but are reminiscent of old colonial Bahamian homes.
The new developers are big on preservation and the environment, so the resort is just a small footprint on the island, leaving beaches as pristine as when they arrived.

SPAS

The Spa at Kamalame Cay

Kamalame Cay, Staniard Cay, Andros. 242-368-6281 or 1-800-790-7971. www.kamalame.com.

For true relaxation, book a treatment at the Spa at Kamalame Cay. Therapists use Biotropica oils and lotions to pamper body and soul. After a long day in the sun, the Cool-As-a-Cucumber Wrap is truly refreshing and therapeutic. The spa menu includes a full range of wraps, massages and facials.
If you're not staying on the resort, allow extra time for the ferry ride from the mainland to the Cay.

Spa Chakra

Bimini Bay Resort and Marina, North Bimini. 242-347-2900. www.biminibayresort.com.

Opened in December 2008, this luxury spa practices the Guerlain Méthode and doesn't use any electronic equipment. There are six deluxe treatment rooms, plus a full-service salon.

BEACHES

If pristine beaches absent of jet skis, music and even other people are what you're looking for, then Andros, The Berry Islands and Bimini are where you need to go. The coastlines of the many islands in this grouping are lined with incredible white sand beaches and stretch for miles. Coral reefs just off the coast make them perfect for a day of snorkeling.

Private Island Paradise

Norwegian Cruise Lines and its passengers are only the latest to use Great Stirrup Cay. Originally home to Arawak Indians and later pirates, who used it as a safe haven while plundering Spanish ships laden with treasure. During the American Civil War, Great Stirrup Cay was used for provisions for federal troops and during the second world war, the troops moved in, making the little island a base to help guard the east coast of the United States. The lighthouse was erected in 1863 and is now solar powered, flashing on a timer. Part of the Berry Island chain, the Cay is owned by the cruise line and is exclusively for their use.

Summer Set Beach★

Two miles south of Fresh Creek, Andros.

You'll have to wait until low tide to realize why this stretch of sand is a favorite in Andros.
Similar to the many other beaches along the eastern coast of the island, Summer Set Beach, so called for the hundreds of little sunset-colored shells strewn across the sand, becomes extremely wide when the tide goes out.

Alice Town Trio

Alice Town, North Bimini.

Bimini may be one of the smallest islands in the Bahama chain, but it's got beaches a plenty.
The most popular are the three beaches that meld into one another at Alice Town. Blister Beach,

Beach on Andros

©2005 Lars Topelmann/The Bahamas Ministry of Tourism

Radio Beach and Spook Hill are definitely worthy of a visit.

Haines Cay Beach

Haines Cay, Berry Islands.

Separated from Great Harbour Cay by a narrow creek, Haines Cay's 3½ mile beach that lines the entire coast is a shell seeker's treasure trove. A sand bank emerges at low tide, dotted with sand dollars and star fish.

Sugar Beach

Great Harbour Cay, Berry Islands.

Step onto this eight-mile long beach and it's clear to see why Great Harbour Cay was once a favorite tropical playground for Hollywood royalty like Cary Grant and Brigitte Bardot. Sugar Beach still retains its appeal as a secluded spot to spend a day.

MUSEUMS

These islands have played an important role in the country's development, but sadly, as yet there are few places showcasing their history.

Bimini Museum

King's Highway, Bimini, 242-347 3038. www.bimini-museum.org. Open Mon–Sat 9am–9pm, Sun noon–9pm. $2.

With just one small room occupying the upstairs of a building that's also home to the island's library, don't expect a major collection. That said, they've amassed interesting, and sometimes odd, items and old photographs that somehow tell Bimini's story. Over the years, the islands have been a playground for celebrities, a key player in the bootleg smuggling days of US prohibition, a top deep sea fishing locale and, according to locals, the inspiration for the late Martin Luther King. It turns out he worked on his Nobel Peace Prize acceptance speech while vacationing on the island.
The museum has on display his Bahamian immigration card.

Other items of notable interest include a podium once used by former Bahamian Prime Minister Sir Lynden Pindling and the last British flag to fly over Bimini's government buildings prior to independence in 1973.

Ernest Hemingway

Bimini's beauty and culture have been memorialised in the novels of one of the island's best known visitors. Ernest Hemingway fell in love with Bimini and made the island his summer home in the 1930s.

Bimini was featured prominently in his fictitious classic *Islands in the Stream*, which was published in 1970 after his death. Sadly, the only memorial to Bimini's most famous second home resident was destroyed when the Compleat Angler Hotel burned to the ground in 2006.

PARKS AND GARDENS

With so few people occupying such a large land mass, Andros has long been a safe haven for native wildlife to live and reproduce.
The Big Yard is also prime hunting ground, but recent stringent regulations have ensured the sport is carried out in a sustainable fashion.

Central Andros National Park

Central Andros. Open access.
No admission fee.

Back in 2002, nearly 300,000 acres of land in the center of this sprawling island were set aside for preservation.
As is the case with all other National Parks in the country, this one is managed by the Bahamas National Trust.
The Central Andros National Park includes blue holes, coral reefs, mangrove wetlands and large sections of the expansive pine forest. Many creatures make their home within the park and it's also an important feeding ground for flamingos and other native birds. Because it secures critical habitats for conch and land crabs, both integral to the Bahamian diet, this park plays a key role in sustainable development.

Green Cay Bird Colony

Big Green Cay, Fresh Creek, Andros.

Thanks to great conservation efforts on the part of the Bahamas National Trust and its international partners, Big Green Cay has become the second-largest breeding colony of white-crowned pigeons in the world. As many as ten thousand pairs have been counted here.
Pigeons nest in May and breed in June through September. Because they are a popular prey for hunters, the government enacted stringent laws banning foreigners in the country for less than three months from hunting the pigeon; it also pushed the opening date of hunting season for the white crowned pigeon back a few weeks.
Ask your hotel to organise bird watching and ecotours during your stay.

Rock Iguana on Andros

©Bahamas Tourist Office

NATURAL SITES

To see the best of what these islands have to offer, chances are you're going to have to get on a boat or traipse through the bush. Andros, The Berry Islands and Bimini are wonderful places to get in touch with nature and see some spectacular natural phenomena as you do.

Wood Carving

In addition to the sea, Andros artisans have turned to the land for supplies and inspiration. Award-winning wood carver Henry Wallace can be found chipping away at a piece of native wood in Red Bay. Eventually, his work produces a bonefish or even a mythical Chickcharnie. Wallace and his apprentices practice sustainable art, using dead trees, limbs and driftwood.

Blue Hole

Hoffman's Cay, Berry Islands.

About 30 minutes by boat from Great Harbour Cay lies a true Bahamian oasis.
This blue hole once explored by Jacques Cousteau, is about the circumference of a baseball field and is said to be 600ft deep. There's a natural diving platform on one side about 25ft above the crystal clear water.

Fountain of Youth

South Bimini (or so they say…).

Whether this legendary rejuvenating spring is real or not remains up for debate. Ponce de Leon visited Bimini in 1513 on his search for the fountain said to restore a person's youth, but never did find it.
Ask around in South Bimini and you'll be sure to find a local guide willing to take you to the spot where the spring supposedly once bubbled.

Lost City of Atlantis

©The Bahamas Ministry of Tourism

Lost City of Atlantis

Bimini Bay, Bimini.

You don't have to be a master scuba diver to experience this submerged site.
The large limestone blocks were first discovered in 1968 and many believe they are part of a road once leading to the mythical Lost City of Atlantis. Opinions abound over what this perfectly lined up row of rocks just 20ft below the ocean's surface may or may not be. In recent years, it's been unofficially renamed "Bimini Road."

HISTORIC SITES

Sponging was once a flourishing industry for the Bahamas, but over-harvesting led to its decline. The 'Big Yard' (as locals call Andros) is where you can still see this activity continue.

Androsia Batik Factory

Fresh Creek, Andros. 242-368-2020. www.androsia.com. Open Mon–Fri 9am–5pm. No admission fee.

The brilliant primary- and pastel-colored fabrics created by the Androsia factory have become a symbol of Bahamiana and you can pop in for a tour of the factory. When the company first opened in 1973, women sat on the beach and created the designs using candle wax. Today, the work is done on a much larger scale, but they still use wax and cut sponges to put their stamp on the fabrics before loading the bolts into huge vats of dye.

Designs range from sand dollars and sea shells or fish, turtles and birds. Scraps are handed over to other local artisans to incorporate into their creations.

Sponging and Weaving Straw

Red Bays, North Andros.

This small settlement close to the northwestern coast of Andros is unique in many ways.

The residents there are descendents of the Seminole Indians who fled Florida in the 17th and 18th centuries. With little much else in the way of commerce, the people of Red Bay have created their own industries to eke out a living.

Red Bays is the modern day sponging capital of the Bahamas. In fact, it's one of the few places where this trade is continued.

The sponges are dived out of the ocean, then laid on exposed coral to dry for a week. Then, they're ready to be sorted, boxed and shipped off to market.

Red Bay is also known for a unique straw weaving style. The Palmyra leaves are so tightly woven that baskets and jugs can hold water.

Androsia Batik Factory

WATERSPORTS

With the world's third longest **barrier reef★★★** just off the coast, Andros is a diver's dream. Throughout these northwestern islands you'll find reefs, blue holes and unique wrecks lying on the ocean floor to explore. These islands have long attracted visitors in search of world class conditions for bonefishing and big game fishing.

Dive Sites

Andros Barrier Reef★★★

Eastern coast of Andros.

About 1½ miles off the eastern Andros coastline lies the world's third-largest barrier reef. Measuring 142 miles from north to south, the Andros Barrier Reef is teeming with fish, corals and sea fans. This reef provides a true barrier, separating the island of Andros from the Tongue of the Ocean's fearsome 6,000 foot depths. The variety of sea creatures you can see here is absolutely staggering. One study of a single 10ft diameter head of coral found 18 different types of fish, from the beautifully colorful French Angelfish and Stoplight Parrotfish to tasty snapper and grunts. On the same coral head, there were also 18 varieties of sea fans, sponges and corals. There are a range of **dive and snorkel sights** either in the sheltered waters of the reef, or for the more adventurous, the eerie depths over the wall.

Conch Sound Blue Hole

Conch Sound, Andros.

World diving records have been set in this ocean cavern. The current record is 3,800ft, set in 1994 by American cave diver, Brian Kakuk. He placed his American flag 100ft beyond the British flag left by the previous record holder in 1982. At the start of the dive is an old fishing boat thought to have been sucked in by the strong current. Along the way you'll pass schools of grunts and snapper and the walls of the cave are lined with lobster and crabs.

Reefs around Andros

© 2005 Lars Topelmann/The Bahamas Ministry of Tourism

Stargate Blue Hole

South Andros, near Congo Town.

Just getting to this inland blue hole is an adventure. Accessible only by plane, the mouth of the blue hole is concealed from above by a grotto.

The stalactite formations lining the cave walls are incredible. A National Geographic documentary detailing the collection of stalactites to study the ice ages was filmed here.

Tongue of the Ocean

Eastern coast of Andros.

The Tongue of the Ocean is one of the water features that makes Andros such a popular dive spot. Divers 'drop over the wall' in the deep ocean trench that plunges to more than 6,000ft below the surface. Night dives are particularly spectacular.

All along the wall of Tongue are ledges at varying heights and depths. The rock formations are thought to have been created as the sea level rose and fell during the last ice age.

Satellite photos taken from space clearly show this unusual ocean formation. Its deep blue color stands out visibly from the aquamarine hues surrounding it.

Since the 1960s, the United States has used the Tongue of the Ocean as a testing grounds for anti-submarine warfare using live targets. The Atlantic Undersea Testing and Evaluation Center (AUTEC) is based in Andros Town.

Mamma Rhoda Rock

Off Chub Cay, Berry Islands.

This rock is in quite shallow waters compared to many other popular dive sites, and although it's a boater's nightmare, it's a dream for both scuba divers and snorkelers. The 15ft-high staghorn coral reefs give this site an underwater garden effect.

Bimini Road

Bimini Bay, Bimini.

The large limestone rocks, partially submerged in the ocean floor, are thought to be part of the mythical Lost City of Atlantis.

No other remains have ever been unearthed to give credence to this school of thought, but it's a simple, fun dive with schools of fish swimming along the underwater roadway.

Locals gave it the name "Bimini Road" for its perfectly aligned rows.

Moray Alley

South Bimini.

So named for the abundance of eels living among the coral reef heads, Moray Alley is also home to schools of tropical fish and a variety of coral.

The best sites here are at depths of about 75ft, and for experienced divers it's a wonderful option for a night dive.

Dive Operators

If you intend to dive on the islands of Andros or Bimini, your best bet is to choose a resort that specializes in diving.

On the **Berry Islands**, ask around and you will find somewhere to

113

rent equipment from, although diving is less established here. *You can find more information about the following highly-recommended operators in our Resorts and Spas section (see p 102).*

Andros

Small Hope Bay Lodge 242-368-2014, www.smallhope.com; **Kamalame Cay** 242-368-6281 or 1-800-790-7971, www.kamalame.com.

Bimini Islands

Bill & Nowdla Keefe's Bimini Undersea, **Bimini Big Game Resort and Yacht Club** 242-347-3391or 1-800-737-1007, www.biminibiggame.com; **Scuba Bimini Dive Resort** 954-524-6090, www.scubabimini.com.

🐟 Bonefishing

Bonefish tend to migrate toward shallow, clear waters and Andros, Bimini and the Berry Islands have a plethora of such places. Andros is regarded as the "bonefishing capital of the world," and while divers spend most of their time on the eastern side, those fishermen hoping to catch the ghost of the flats spend their days on the northwestern coast.

Bonefishing isn't big with the local set, but many Bahamians make a living taking tourists to the hot spots. These local guides figured out the benefits of sustainable tourism a long time ago and practice catch and release fishing to ensure there are bonefish in the area for generations to come.

As for where the best spots are, well that depends entirely on the tides, the weather and, well, the fish. Your best bet is to hire one of the top notch bonefishing guides to take you out for a day or half day of fishing.

They seem to have an uncanny knack for knowing just where to go on a given day. Arrange a guide with your hotel, or give one of the guides listed a call *(see p 115)*. Rates range from $250 for a half day to $450 for a full day of fishing.

🐟 Big Game Fishing

If Andros is known as the "Bonefishing Capital of the World," then Bimini has surely earned its reputation as "Big Game Fishing Capital of the World." Ernest Hemingway was an avid angler who helped

Bonefishing in Andros

© 2005 Lars Topelmann/The Bahamas Ministry of Tourism

MUST DO

Game fishing in Bimini

Bonefishing Guides & Charter Captains

Bonefishing

Andros - Marvin Miller (Mangrove Cay) 242-329-2484; Rodney "Andros Angler" Miller (Pleasant Harbour, North Andros) 242-329 2039; Ralph Moxey (Little Harbour, Mangrove Cay) 242-69-0218; Prescott Smith (Stafford Creek) 242-368-6050; Stanley Forbes (Congo Town) 242-369-4767; Seascape Inn (Mangrove Cay, Andros) 242-369-0342, www.seascapeinn. com

Berry Islands - Joel Darville (Little Harbour) 242-464-4198; Percy Darville (Great Harbour Cay) 242-464-4149; Anthony "Shoes" Pinder (Great Harbour Cay) 242-464-4173.

Bimini - Ansil "Bonefish Ansil" Saunders 242-347-2178 or 242-464-5113; Ebbie David (Alice Town) 242-347-2053; Raymond Pritchard (Bailey Town) 242-347-2269.

Deep Sea Fishing

Andros - Small Hope Bay (Andros Island) 242-368-2014.

Berry Islands - Anthony Pinder (Great Harbour Cay) 242-464-4173; Berry Island Club (Fraizer's Hog Cay) 1-800-933-3533; Five Hearts Enterprises (Bullocks' Harbour & Great Harbour Cay) 242-464-4149

Bimini - Captain Frank Hinzey 242-347 3072; Captain Jerome Stuart 242-347-2081; Captain Al Sweeting 242-347-3477.

get the word out about the amazing fishing grounds surrounding the tiny islands that make up the Bimini chain.

Just 50 miles from Florida's east coast, Bimini is an ideal quick getaway for those bringing their own boats across, but if you fly in, there are local captains who charter boats for day trips.

Whether you're a serious fisherman or just looking for a fun time, you've got a good chance of reeling in marlin, tuna, dolphin and wahoo.

Berry Islands: Best of Both

The Berry Islands don't have a grand title to boast about, but in this case, playing second fiddle isn't a bad thing.

You can fish the Tongue of the Ocean for Blue Marlin, dolphin, Sailfish, Shark, Tuna and Wahoo one day, and the next, hit the flats in search of that elusive bonefish, tarpum or permit.

WATERSPORTS

ABACOS: GREAT ABACOS, LITTLE ABACOS

The Abacos are a chain of islands and cays in the northern Bahamas with a rich history dating back to the days when new Americans sought refuge during the American Revolution.

Great Abaco: Marsh Harbour & Treasure Cay

The small city of Marsh Harbour is the economic heartbeat of the Abacos. Situated in the middle of Great Abaco, Marsh Harbour serves as the perfect hub for the surrounding cays. This is the place to stock up on groceries and stop at the bank. The yachting crowd flocks to the area's many marinas, and even land-based visitors tend to rent small boats, and head off for a day of cay hopping. If you're not comfortable navigating the shallow seas on your own, small ferries operate throughout the day, linking the islands. Farther north is Treasure Cay. The settlement's name is deceptive, as it's actually part of the mainland. It's clear that the small city center developed around the main resort here in order to provide land and water-based visitors with all the ameni-

ties they need. Treasure Cay's 3½-mile stretch of sandy beach has been consistently ranked one of the top ten in the world.

Hope Town, Man O'War, Green Turtle Cay & Great Guana Cay

Nice as the mainland is, it's the cays off the eastern coast that make Abaco so special, and they all have a different flavor. Hope Town is called "Hollywood" by locals because it's the place to be and be seen, while Man O'War retains much of the Puritan values of days gone by and bans the sale of liquor. The cays are small enough to stroll around the main settlements, but tooling around in a golf cart is a fun way to go. Perfect as day trips, many visitors want to spend more time, and the cays have a variety of hotels and B&Bs to choose from.

Windsurfing at Treasure Cay

MUST SEE ABACOS

©The Bahamas Ministry of Tourism

Rental golf cart

©The Bahamas Ministry of Tourism

Getting Around

The proximity of the cays to the mainland makes exploring easy. *See p 126* for boat rental options.

By Golf cart: *Guana Cay Rentals – Guana Cay (242-365-5195); Island Cart Rentals – Hope Town (242-366-0448); Island Treasures – Man O'War (242-365-6072); Resort Cart Rentals – Treasure Cay (242-365-8771); Sea Side Cart Rentals – Green Turtle Cay (242-365-4147)*.

By Car: *Cornish Car Rental – Treasure Cay (242-365-8623); Quality Star Car Rentals – Marsh Harbour (242-367-2979).* **By Ferry**: *Albury's Ferry (242-367-3147) connecting Marsh Harbour to Great Guana Cay, Hope Town and Man O'War; Green Turtle Ferry (242-365-4166) connecting Treasure Cay to Green Turtle Cay.*

RESORTS

There are no mega resorts in the Abacos. Quaint island-style hotels and historic B&Bs are more the flavor. That said, most know what it takes to cater to a discerning clientele and offer upscale furnishings, complete amenities, and at many, there's property-wide Wi-Fi so you can keep in touch while lounging poolside. For more information and to find hotels not part of major resorts see *Must Stay*.

$$$$$	over $650		**$$**	$100–$250
$$$$	$400–$650		**$**	under $100
$$$	$250–$400			

Mermaid Reef

$$$$$ **4 rooms**
Pelican Shores, Marsh Harbour. 242-367-0518. www.mermaid reef.com.

This small resort is comprised of four two-bedroom villas. Rooms are outfitted with sunken whirlpool bathtubs, king size beds and a fully equipped kitchen. A short drive away from the main drag of hotels and restaurants in Marsh Harbour, guests here enjoy true solitude and magnificent views whether they spend their time on the private manmade beach, sitting by the freshwater pool or on their villa balcony.

Abaco Beach Resort and Boat Harbour

$$$$ **92 rooms**
Bay Street, Marsh Harbour, Great Abaco. 242-367-2158 or 242-367-2736. www.abacoresort.com.

The Abaco Beach Resort is one of the more popular resorts on the mainland, thanks in large part to its expansive marina and private, sandy white beach. It's a hotbed of fun activity during the yachting season and it has a fantastic pool. The bar extends into it and is surrounded by partially submerged

RESORTS

117

bar stools. Rooms are spacious, have balconies overlooking the beach and ocean, and are nicely furnished. For those who simply have to keep in touch, you can access the free Wi-Fi from just about anywhere on the property. Angler's Restaurant overlooks the marina and is one of the more upscale dining options in Marsh Harbour.

Flip Flops on the Beach

$$$ 4 rooms
Great Guana Cay. 242-365-5137 or 1-800-222-2646. www.flipflops onthebeach.com.

Never have flip flops been so elegant. This gem of a resort offers just four luxuriously furnished one- and two-bedroom bungalows, so privacy, peace and quiet are guaranteed. Rooms are decorated with Bahama Handprint fabrics, mahogany four poster beds and 1,000 thread count sheets. Fully appointed kitchens in the two-bedroom bungalows and kitchenettes in the one-bedrooms are perfect for longer stays on island. If you're not interested in cooking, head five minutes down the beach to Nipper's Beach Bar & Grill. Their Sunday afternoon pig roast is legendary and attracts locals and visitors from all over the Abacos.

Bluff House Beach Hotel and Yacht Club

$$ 36 rooms
Green Turtle Cay. 242-365-4247 or 1-800-745-4911. www.bluff house.com.

This upscale resort claims to be the oldest in the Family Islands, and with panoramic views of Green Turtle Cay, the Sea of Abaco, White Sound and the Atlantic Ocean from the wrap around deck at the main house at Bluff House, it's clear to see why it's still around. Once you get outside of New Plymouth proper, roads turn into dirt tracks, so although you can get to Bluff House by car or golf cart, it's reached most easily by boat. Villas and suites dot the hillside overlooking White Sound, while the beautiful rainbow of yachtsman's cottages line the marina. All rooms have water views, and the cottages include private decks with an outdoor Jacuzzi.

Dolphin Beach Resort

© The Bahamas Ministry of Tourism

Dolphin Beach Resort

$$ 22 rooms
Great Guana Cay. 242-365-5137 or 1-800-222-2646. www.dolphin beachresort.com.

Brightly colored cottages dot the landscape overlooking the incredible miles-long stretch of beach. Each is unique in design and size inside and out. One has a swinging bed and is dubbed the honeymoon suite. Another has a loft accessible by ladder that's popular with teens, and yet another includes a room outfitted with bunkbeds for younger kids. Just 50ft off the shore lies the

Great Abaco **Barrier Reef★★★**, so grab a mask and snorkel and go exploring. If you're looking for a less strenuous way to while away the day, ask the front desk to set up your beach chairs and umbrella, sit back and relax.

Green Turtle Club

$$ 31 rooms
Green Turtle Cay. 242-365-4271 or 1-866-528-0539. www.greenturtle club.com.

Green Turtle Club is a bit of a golf cart ride from historic New Plymouth, but the picturesque town can be seen from the property's small beach across tranquil White Sound. In addition to a small, private beach on site, the property is walking distance from some of the island's most stunning Atlantic side beaches. Rooms are elegantly appointed with mahogany four poster beds and furnishings, and French-inspired draperies and linens. As peaceful as the beach

Green Turtle Club

© The Bahamas Ministry of Tourism

may be, the hottest hangout spot on this property is the English pub-style bar and lounge next to the dining room. On cooler winter evenings, guests gather around a log fire to share tales of the day's adventures.

Abaco Inn

$ 22 rooms
White Sound, Hope Town, Elbow Cay. 242-366-0133 or 1-800-468-8799. www.abacoinn.com.

After getting the ferry over to Hope Town, you'll be whisked away by golf cart to this serene resort nestled amid sand dunes and palm trees. Rooms have a definite family island feel, with pickled wood panel walls.
Each room, whether it's a bungalow or luxury villa, has a stunning view of either the Sea of Abaco or the Atlantic Ocean. Many rooms have a private porch and just steps away, your own personal hammock—perfect for an afternoon nap.

Conch Inn Resort and Marina

$ 9 rooms
Bay Street, Marsh Harbour, Great Abaco. 242-367-4000 or 242-367-4003. www.conchinn.com.

More marina than resort, this property is conveniently located smack in the middle of Marsh Harbour's happening restaurant and hotel row. The nine rooms in the simple, single-story building overlook a garden terrace and the harbour marina. There's no direct access to a beach, but Marsh Harbour is small enough that beautiful beaches are never far away.

RESORTS

Treasure Cay Resort

©The Bahamas Ministry of Tourism

Treasure Cay Resort

$ 93 rooms
*Treasure Cay, Great Abaco.
242-365-8801 or 1-800-327-1584.
www.treasurecay.com.*

This sprawling property on a peninsula about a half-hour drive north of Marsh Harbour came first, and the town that now surrounds it came later.

Rooms are housed in a three-story pastel-colored complex and have views of a lush tropical garden or the marina. Suites have a private balcony overlooking the marina. A short walk along the marina and across the main road that leads through Treasure Cay takes you to one of the most beautiful stretches of beach anywhere in the world. In fact, the 3½-mile long beach has been ranked one of the top ten anywhere.

Over the years, a small town has emerged, offering hotel and marina guests all the comforts of home including a well-stocked foodstore, bank, liquor store and Café Le Florence serving up fresh baked world famous cinnamon rolls each morning.

Rental Houses

Abaco Estate Services—*Treasure Cay, 242-365-8752, www.abaco estateservices.com;* **Abaco Vacation Planner**—*Marsh Harbour, Guana Cay, 242-367-3529, www. abacovacationplanner.com;* **Green Turtle Rentals,** *Green Turtle Cay, 242-365-4120, www. greenturtlerentals.com;* **Hope Town Hideaways**, *Hope Town, 242-366-0224, www.hopetown. com.*

The Lazy Lizard… Peace 'n' Rice… Abaco Rum Cake… The names of Abaco's many rental homes and cottages are as alluring as their design. Turnkey houses that can comfortably accommodate a family or a group of friends are ideal for longer visits. Most require a minimum week-long stay, and chances are, you'll wish you could stay even longer. Some prime properties are booked years out, so be sure to start vacation home hunting early.

HISTORIC BUILDINGS

With a history dating back to the end of the American Revolution, the Abaco cays still boast many examples of original Loyalist Saltbox homes. They've withstood devastating hurricanes and held up to the beating Bahama sunshine for the past 150 or more years, and many Abaonians still call them home.

Hope Town Lighthouse★

Hope Town Harbour. Open to the public. No admission fee.
Ask ferry boat captain about drop off and pick up.

This red and white candy-striped lighthouse is, without a doubt, one of the most photographed structures in the Bahamas. Rising 120ft tall, it makes picking Hope Town out from the smattering of other nearby cays easy. While it is loved for the charm it adds today, Hope Town residents fought the construction in the mid-1800s, as it brought an end to their lucrative ship wrecking and salvaging industry.

Today, it's one of the only lighthouses left in the world to ward off ships with a kerosene powered light which flashes every 15 seconds. The lighthouse keeper is on duty most weekdays and is always happy to give visitors a look. The views make the 100-step climb to the top well worth the effort.

Chamberlain Kendrick House

Walter Street, Green Turtle Cay.

After years of neglect, this weathered two-story wooden home isn't much to look at, but its history makes it worth a peek. When he was a young boy, former British Prime Minister (1937–1940) Neville Chamberlain called it home. His father owned a sisal plantation in the islands and brought the family over for years. The house is still owned by the family of the medical missionary who purchased it from the Chamberlains.

Green Turtle Cay Cemetery

Parliament & Victoria Streets, Green Turtle Cay. Open 24 hours.

Modern residents of this small, tight-knit community are buried alongside their ancestors in this beautifully maintained water-side cemetery. The oldest tomb-stone inscription dates back to 1830, but many have been eroded over the centuries and it's believed there are graves dating back to 1790. The southeast corner of the

©The Bahamas Ministry of Tourism
Hope Town Lighthouse

graveyard was originally used for cholera victims and to this date remains unused for others.

A few blocks away, on Crown Street, is a one-room white with green trim building aptly named Coffin House. Built in 1937, it's where the New Plymouth Burial Society stores its caskets.

The Lighthouse (Hole-in-the-Wall)

Hole in the Wall, Great Abaco. No admission fee.

To say getting to this southern point lighthouse is an adventure is an understatement.

From Marsh Harbour, it's a good 45 minute or longer drive along a well-maintained highway bisecting the Abaco pine forests. About 10 miles past the settlement of Crossing Rocks is a sign for the Abaco National Park *(www.bnt. bs/parks_abaco)*—a protected track of pine forest, home to the Bahama Parrot. Continue along a pot-holed dirt track road to the tiny settlement of Hole in the Wall. It's the end of the line in Abaco, but home to the island grouping's lesser known and lesser visited red and white lighthouse. There's not much there, and the ground is uneven, so be sure to pack water and snacks and wear sturdy shoes for the trip.

The Old Gaol

© The Bahamas Ministry of Tourism

The Old Gaol

Parliament & Victoria Streets, Green Turtle Cay.

It's ironic that a point of interest on Green Turtle Cay is the old derelict jailhouse, considering the island is crime-free today and doesn't have a modern facility to house criminals.

The single-story structure that remains is not the original jail. First built in the early 1800s, the two-story complex housed the jail on the ground floor and upstairs was the post office and commissioner's office. The 1932 hurricane which washed away 75 percent of the island's buildings destroyed the original structure and it was rebuilt in shortly after. The building remains boarded up, but the gates surrounding the property are left unlocked so visitors can take a peek. The building houses three jail cells with peephole slots. Two smaller buildings on the property house additional cells and a bathroom. Stairs to the upstairs that no longer exists remain in place.

ABACOS

MUST SEE

MUSEUMS AND GALLERIES

Modern day Abaconians are proud of their Loyalist heritage and demonstrate it with a smattering of historical museums where art, artifacts, newspaper clippings and other items are proudly displayed.

Albert Lowe Museum★

Parliament Street, Green Turtle Cay. 242-365-4094. Open Mon–Sat 9am–11:45am and 1pm–4pm. $5, children $2.50.

The tour through Green Turtle Cay's history is a steal at just $5. As she walks you through the exhibits, local historian Miss Ivy stops to point out the house where her mother was born, or the cottage her uncle re-built after the infamous 1932 hurricane that destroyed most of the island. Quite honestly, what Miss Ivy doesn't know about Green Turtle Cay's fascinating history simply isn't worth knowing.

The 150-year-old Loyalist Saltbox house with porch is an artifact in itself. The museum is named after the late Albert Lowe—one of the island's best known ship builders. Bedrooms and a bathroom up the steep flight of stairs are maintained in the style they would have been decorated when the house was first built.

And a short walk away from the main house in the back garden is a free-standing kitchen that's also stood still over the past century. Prints of paintings done by Albert's son, Alton Lowe, are available for sale as are copies of books about the Bahamas.

Johnston's Foundry & Gallery

Little Harbour, Great Abaco. 242-366-3503. Open 10am–noon and 2pm–4pm.

Throughout the tiny harborside community of Little Harbour, you'll stumble across sea creatures cast in bronze. They were hand cast by the Johnston family who've been working their craft since settling here and starting the neighborhood in 1951.

Local lore has it that their first home was one of the caves across the protected harbor.

Watch them at work on new pieces and check out some of their stunning creations in the gallery next door. The most famous works were created by the original Johnston—Randolph. He designed the bust of the Bahamas'

Albert Lowe Museum

©The Bahamas Ministry of Tourism

first Governor General, Sir Milo Butler, that adorns Rawson Square in **Nassau★**, as well as The Seven Ages of Man piece that is housed in the local gallery.

Once you're done there, pop on over to Pete's Pub *(242-366-3503; www.petespub.com)* where you're guaranteed a cold drink, a good bite and an interesting conversation with one of the local characters who call Little Harbour home.

Wyannie Malone Historical Museum

Queen's Highway, Hope Town, Elbow Cay. 242-366-0293. www.hopetownmuseum.com. Opening hours depend on volunteer availability. A sign is usually posted on the door.

This museum, established in 1978, is named after the original matriarch of Hope Town, Wyannie Malone, a widower from South Carolina who sought refuge in the Abacos after the American Revolution. She, along with her four young children, was the first to call Hope Town home.

The museum is set up to accurately depict an authentic Loyalist home, and is packed with artifacts and information about Hope Town through the ages.

For a walking tour of historic Hopetown, contact Debbie Malone *(242-367-0646)*, an eighth-generation descendant of Wyannie Malone. She conducts tours every Tuesday and Thursday. Meet at the post office just a few doors down from the museum. *Costs $10 per person.*

Wyannie Malone Historical Museum

© The Bahamas Ministry of Tourism

PARKS AND GARDENS

Small gardens, most created to pay tribute to Abaconians who helped develop the community, tend to be quite simple and take just a few minutes to wander around, but park benches and shady trees often make them a nice break from the hot sun.

Abaco National Park

Ten miles past Crossing Rocks, heading south. No admission fee.

In 1994, the Bahamian government agreed to create a 20,500-acre National Park in South Abaco, managed by the Bahamas National Trust. The park, which is easily accessible, includes 5,000 acres of pine forest.

Early morning birders can catch a glimpse of a number of other birds including West Indian Woodpeckers, Bahama Swallows, Bahama Yellowthroats, Loggerhead Kingbirds, Olive-capped Warblers and Bahama Mockingbirds. The national forest also includes a nesting habitat for Bahama Parrots.

Bahama Parrot in Abaco National Park

© The Bahamas Ministry of Tourism

Abaco's Healing Tree

Whatever it is that ails you, chances are the folks at Abaco Neem have a solution. The **Neem tree** is native to India, but a local planted a farm and set up a factory to make teas, salves, capsules, lotions and other products. Neem is said to help with skin problems, boost immune systems and minimize the effects of arthritis. *Marsh Harbour. 242-367-4117. www.abaconeem.com.*

There is a great effort underway to boost the population of this endangered species.

Check with the Ministry of Tourism office *(242-367-3067)* in Marsh Harbour about securing a local guide. Be sure to dress appropriately: wear sturdy shoes and take bug repellent.

Memorial Sculpture Garden

Parliament Street, Green Turtle Cay. Open 24 hours. Donations welcomed.

American artist James Mastin was commissioned to design these busts of famous Bahamians—some still living. The garden was created in 1983 to commemorate the bicentennial anniversary of the arrival of the Loyalists to Abaco. The bronze sculptures are mounted on native coral bases.

The centerpiece sculpture is of two young women—one a Loyalist and the other a young woman of African descent.

It's hard to tell from ground level, but the garden pathways are laid out in the design of the Union Jack—the British flag.

Memorial Sculpture Garden

© The Bahamas Ministry of Tourism

WATERSPORTS

To come to the Abacos and not spend time enjoying the magnificent water would be a crime. Superb snorkeling spots that you can just walk off the beach to, incredible dive sites and beaches that make international top-ten lists make this a water lover's paradise.

Boating and Sailing

The sheltered harbors and many accessible cays make the Abacos a prime destination for bareboating—sailing unassisted.

There are plenty of options for marinas, and if you're not lucky enough to cruise in on your own boat, then Marsh Harbour is where you'll find a vast range of rentals. Whether you're looking for a dinghy, a powerboat, or a state-of-the-art yacht, you will find it here, although you will have to book ahead.

If you're not an experienced sailor you can charter a sailboat with the crew, or book one of the many popular island cruises through your hotel.

Marinas

Club Soleil Marina—*Hope Town, 242-366-0003, www.clubsoleil. com/marina. 16 slip marina;* **Conch Inn Marina**—*Marsh Harbour, 242-367-4000, www.conch*

inn.com/marina. 80 slip marina; **Bluff House Yacht Club**—*Green Turtle Cay, 242-365-4247 or 1-800-745-4911, www.bluffhouse.com. 40 slip marina.*

 Boat Rentals

JIC Boat Rentals—*Treasure Cay, 242-365-8582, www.jicboatrentals com;* **Sea Horse Boat Rentals** — *Marsh Harbour, www.sea-horse. com, 242-367-2513;* **Rich's Rentals**—*Marsh Harbour, www. richsrental.com, 242-367-2682.*

Bonefishing

Ronnie Sawyer—*Green Turtle Cay, 242-365-4070 or 242-357-6667;* **Pete & Gay Guest House**—*Sandy Point, 242-366-4119;* **Buddy Pinder**—*Marsh Harbour, 242-366-2163;* **Junior Albury**—*Cherokee Sound, 242-366-3058.*

Unless you're looking for frustration, your best bet for finding the ghost of the flats' is to hire one of the scores of local guides.

These men have decades of experience and know the best flats and understand the local tide flows to ensure you have the best chance of spotting or catching one of the elusive bonefish.

Settlements like Sandy Point and Cherokee Sound are world famous for bonefishing and this sport sustains many who live here.

The best spot the Abacos has to

Sailing in the Abacos

© The Bahamas Ministry of Tourism

offer is called the "Marls." Located on the western side of the mainland, this 400 square mile area of flats is where you'll be most likely to find a bonefish worthy of a photograph.

Although bonefish is a tasty treat worth picking through all the bones, most of the islands' fishermen practice catch and release to ensure the industry is around for generations to come.

Deep Sea Fishing

The Rock Fishing Trips—*Green Turtle Cay, 242-365-4069 or 242-357-6784;* **Robert Lowe**—*Hope Town, 242-366-0266.*

There's no better dinner than fresh fish, and it's better still if you caught it yourself.
There are some great fishing grounds off the Abacos coast. Depending on the season (and a little bit of luck) you can haul blue marlin, swordfish, dolphin and grouper.

Diving

Brendal's Dive Center—*Green Turtle Cay, 242-365-4411, www.brendal.com;* **Dive Abaco**—*Marsh Harbour, 242-367-2787, www.diveabaco.com;* **Froggies Out Island Adventure**—*Hope Town, 242-366-0431, www.froggiesabaco.com;* **Treasure Divers**—*Treasure Cay, 242-365-8571, www.treasure-divers.com.*

Just off the coast of Abaco lie some incredible dive sites at a variety of depths, from Eagle Ray Pass at 25ft to the 65ft Black Tip Alley and The Ledge at 100ft and beyond.
Come face to face with Abaco's ship wrecking past and dive the Wreck of the San Jacinto, which was the first American steamship made. The ship sank in 1865. Close encounters with sharks are always popular and Abaco doesn't disappoint. If that's too adventurous for you, instructors will be happy to introduce you to their less intimidating 'pet' groupers, turtles and rays.
Don't worry if you're not certified. Most diver operations offer basic learn to dive courses so you don't have to miss out on the beauty that lies beneath.

Kayaking

Brendal's Dive Center

Green Turtle Cay. 242-365-4411. www.brendal.com.

If you want adventure, but want to do it at a slower pace and stay dry, then rent a kayak and explore the smaller uninhabited cays.

Wild Dolphin Encounters

Brendal's Dive Center—*Green Turtle Cay, 242-365-4411, www.brendal.com;* **Froggies Out Island Adventure**—*Hope Town, 242-366-0431, www.froggiesabaco.com.*

There's no guarantee that the wild dolphins who call the ocean around Abaco home will come out to play on any given day, but there's a good chance. Dive operators offer excursions taking you into the areas where dolphins are known to be, and you can put on your mask, snorkel and fins, hop in and interact with flipper and friends in their natural habitat.

ELEUTHERA, HARBOUR ISLAND & SPANISH WELLS

Idyllic Eleuthera has a laidback ambience that attracts those who are looking for rest and relaxation. It's a 2-mile trip across the water to stunning Harbour Island and you'll find the tightknit community of Spanish Wells at the very Northern tip of Eleuthera.

Eleuthera

Eleuthera got its name, which means 'freedom' from the British subjects fleeing persecution at home. They wrecked off the coast in 1649 and made the island home.

Today, many of their descendents, and the descendents of United States Loyalists from the 1700s, live in small communities on the long and skinny island. Beautiful, untouched beaches dot the landscape of what was once the pineapple growing capital of the world.

Visitors come to dive and snorkel the offshore coral reefs, which are absolutely out of this world. Be sure to also make time for exploring the inland caves and lush green countryside.

Harbour Island & Spanish Wells

In the early-19th century, Harbour Island's **Dunmore Town★** was the second largest in the country. Today, it is one of the country's most picturesque settlements with much of the original Loyalist-style architecture painstakingly preserved.

'Briland', as the locals call it, has become a favorite tropical island getaway for the world's rich and famous, but still maintains a quaint old time feel. It's also where you'll find the world famous **Pink Sands Beach★★**.

Spanish Wells is the wealthiest community in the Bahamas thanks to a booming lobster fishing industry. Spanish Wells is a residential town with little emphasis on tourism, but it's still worth a day visit.

Aerial view of the Glass Window, Eleuthera

ELEUTHERA AND HARBOUR ISLAND

MUST SEE

RESORTS

Harbour Island has long been a home away from home for the rich and famous, so resort owners here have had to step up their game and offer true island luxury. Not to be outdone, there are some real gems to be discovered all along mainland Eleuthera too. For more information and to find hotels not part of major resorts see *Must Stay*.

$$$$$	over $650	$$	$100–$250
$$$$	$400–$650	$	under $100
$$$	$250–$400		

The Blue Bar at Pink Sands Resort

© Peter Brown/Pink Sands Resorts

Cape Eleuthera Resort & Yacht Club

$$$$$ 38 rooms
Rock Sound, Eleuthera. 242-334-8500. www.capeeleuthera.com.

Located on a 9mi long private peninsula, Cape Eleuthera Resort is the island's southernmost upscale resort.
The owners have been trying to shed the former name—Powell Point Resort—without much luck.
Luxury town homes overlook the marina and offer spectacular sunrise and sunset views.
The surrounding area is dotted with secluded beaches perfect for romantic picnics.

Pink Sands Resort

$$$$$ 25 rooms
Chapel Street, Harbour Island. 242-333-2030 or 1-800-407-4776. www.pinksandsresort.com.

Aptly named for its prime location overlooking the world famous **Pink Sands Beach★★**, Pink Sands set the standard for which Harbour Island has come to be known.
The very private one- and two-bedroom cottages are set within an official bird sanctuary, and usually, the only sounds you'll hear as you stroll down the meandering pathway to the beach are the birds chirping and the waves breaking on the shore.

129

All rooms have California King beds and private patios. One of the garden view rooms includes an enclosed courtyard with a Jacuzzi and drench shower. The Blue Bar, where breakfast and lunch are served, offers stunning sunsets overlooking the Atlantic Ocean.

🔥 Rock House

$$$$ 9 rooms
Bay & Hill Street, Harbour Island. 242-333-2053. www.rockhouse bahamas.com.

This adult-only upcscale resort sits atop a limestone ledge overlooking the harbor. No detail has been left out. The swimming pool is heated for year-round comfort and there are luxurious cabanas lining the pool deck. Rooms have top-of-the-line furnishings and amenities and have views of the harbor, garden, or pool.

Rock House is a short golf cart ride from the famous **Pink Sands Beach★★**, and guests can take advantage of the hotel's own spot outfitted with umbrellas and deck chairs. The attentive staff will even pack a cooler for you to take with you.

The Cove

$$$ 26 rooms
Queen's Highway, Gregory Town, Eleuthera. 242-335-5142 or 1-800-552-5960. www.thecove eleuthera.com.

A few years ago, two American couples visited this property, bought it and transformed it into a chic, welcoming, home away from home. Rooms, decorated with sorbet-colored linens, are housed in pods scattered across the property. They are all air conditioned, but feel free to open the windows and sliding glass door and enjoy the cool ocean breeze. There are no televisions or telephones in the rooms, but guests are provided with complimentary ipods® during their stay.

The Cove has two beaches—one of them with pink sand—right outside your door, perfect for lounging on a hammock suspended from twin palms, snorkeling or even kayaking. The hilltop pool is the perfect place to unwind after a long day of doing nothing.

The Landing

$$$ 7 rooms
Bay Street, Harbour Island. 242-333-2707. www.harbourisland landing.com.

The Landing's main building, which houses two guest rooms upstairs and the restaurant and bar downstairs, was constructed in 1800. The other five guest rooms can be found in the Captain's House Building built 20 years later. Situated right along the main street and harbor, The Landing still creates an old world oasis.

The bedrooms were all decorated by Harbour Island resident India Hicks, whose grandfather was Lord Mountbatten.

Room rates include breakfast and free property-wide Wi-Fi. Ask for a tour of Toby's Wine Cellar, carved out of the limestone hill next door and pick your bottle to have with dinner at the exquisite Landing Restaurant.

The beach is a short golf cart ride away, but a pool was recently installed for hotel guests.

Pineapple Fields

$$$ **36 rooms**
Banks Road, between Governors Harbour and Palmetto Point, Eleuthera. 242-332-2221. www.pineapplefields.com.

Eight clapboard cottages containing four condominium-style units overlook the Atlantic Ocean. Units include a bedroom with king size bed and living room with queen size pullout, two private verandas and laundry facilities. Pineapple Fields is a condo-tel, so if you're interested in staying there during the busy season, be sure to book early, otherwise unit owners may just be in residence. Tippys, a beach side bistro next door has earned a reputation of one of the mainland's must-do restaurants.

Beach at Pineapple Fields

©Pineapple Fields

Beach★★ exclusively for use by hotel and marina guests.

Valentines Resort and Marina

$$$ **58 rooms**
Bay Street, Harbour Island. 242-333-2142. www.valentines resort.com.

Completely renovated in 2005, Valentine's is the biggest resort on the island, but the townhouse-style layout ensures guests never feel like one of the crowd. One- and two-bedroom townhouses include fully equipped kitchens or kitchenettes, and large balconies overlooking the pool, gardens, marina and harbor. There's an open layout bar and a full service restaurant on site, and Valentine's 50-slip marina is the largest on the island. The resort has its own spot on Harbour Island's famous **Pink Sands**

Surfers Beach Manor

$ **12 rooms**
Near Hatchet Bay, Eleuthera. 242-335-5300. www.surfers manor.com.

As you'd expect from its name and location, Surfers Beach Manor is a big hit with those hoping to catch a wave on Surfer's Beach. There's nothing fancy about this family-owned and operated hotel, but its comfortable and has all the basic amenities you need for an island vacation. There's no pool, but most guests opt to spend their days on the beach. And if surfing's your thing, this small hotel provides the easiest access to a beach that's not so easy to get to unless you're driving a rugged four wheel drive vehicle or up for a long walk.

RESORTS

131

BEACHES

If ever there were a place where you could be guaranteed to put the first footprints of the day on a sandy beach, Eleuthera is it. Although it's best known for the **Pink Sands Beach**★★ on Harbour Island, the coast of the mainland is peppered with some incredible spots for beaching, shelling, snorkeling and surfing.

Pink Sands Beach★★

Harbour Island, Atlantic side.

This beach consistently makes it on top ten lists and the minute you catch a glimpse of it, you'll understand why.

The hard packed sand stretches 3mi long and hundreds of feet wide, so even if everyone on Harbour Island decided to head on over, this beach still wouldn't be crowded.

Depending on the sun, the sand may not look strikingly pink, but grab a handful and you'll see it really is a different color. The white sand is mixed with tiny pieces of conch shell crushed by the reefs offshore. Because of the offshore reef, the waves are gentle, which makes for great snorkeling. In the afternoons, you can walk or gallop the beach on horseback.

Club Med Beach

Governor's Harbour, Eleuthera, Atlantic side.

The Club Med resort was destroyed by Hurricane Floyd in 1999 and never re-opened, but the pink sand beach still bears its name. Although the water on the Atlantic side of the island tends to be quite rough, Club Med Beach is tucked into a protected cove, so it's an ideal swimming spot but you still get the lovely ocean breeze. Shady casuarina trees are in abundance, but the beach is so wide you'll have quite a walk to take a dip if you put your towel under one.

Small reefs just off the southern and northern ends of the beach are great snorkeling spots.

Club Med Beach

© The Bahamas Ministry of Tourism

Pink Sand in Your Shoes

You don't have to stay on Harbour Island to sink your toes in the famous **Pink Sands Beach**★★. The little island is just two hours away from Nassau via Bahamas Fast Ferries *(242-323-2166; www.bahamasferries.com)*. The Bohengy, with an exposed upper deck and air-conditioned lower deck makes trips once or twice a day depending on the season.

Pink Sands Beach, Harbour Island

New developers are building a resort on the old Club Med site, but the beach remains accessible.

Surfer's Beach

Near Hatchet Bay, Eleuthera, Atlantic side.

This secluded beach is considered one of the best for surfing in the entire Bahamas.
You'll need a four-wheel drive vehicle to make it along the severely pot holed sand road. Otherwise, it's quite a long walk from the highway.
Local surfers have constructed a hilltop lookout complete with hammock chair, and down on the beach there's a shade hut built using driftwood, foam buoys and anything else that's washed ashore.
Because so few bother to make the treacherous trek, there's great shelling.
Head north and you'll come across some rocky formations that contain a natural hot tub. Put on your shoes as the rocks are extremely sharp, and take the plunge.

Ten Bay Beach

Palmetto Point, Eleuthera, Exuma Sound side.

If you're driving along the main highway in Eleuthera, you'll come across beautiful, pristine beaches all along the western coast.
Ten Bay Beach is a perfect place to park your car along the road and take a dip. As with most of the beaches on the island, the only things you can expect to find are seagulls and seashells.

James Point Beach

James Cistern, central Eleuthera, Atlantic side.

Only attempt to access this remote and unspoiled beach in a very reliable 4x4! A bumpy dirt track leads north from the small town toward this idyllic beach, which you will probably have to yourself.
There is a wreck offshore which is great for snorkeling and when the wind is coming from the south, the waves pick up and you can do some surfing too.

BEACHES

NATURAL SITES

Most of the sights in Eleuthera and Harbour Island are off the beaten path, but that only adds to the adventure. With the exception of a possibly haunted mansion, all the sites to see are natural marvels.

The Glass Window

© The Bahamas Ministry of Tourism

The Glass Window★

Queen's Highway, North of Gregory Town, Eleuthera.

You have to get out of your car to truly appreciate this natural wonder, although do be aware that drivers on Eleuthera aren't known for their road safety!

On the eastern side of the bridge the water is a stunning turquoise and usually flat calm. Look to the right and the water is a much deeper blue and the waves of the Atlantic crash against the cliffs. The bridge that links north and south Eleuthera just north of Gregory Town was once a natural rock arch, but it collapsed years ago and has long since been replaced by a manmade structure.

Ocean Hole Rock Sound★

Rock Sound, Eleuthera.
No admission fee.

Even the legendary Jacques Cousteau hasn't been able to figure out where and how this inland lake is linked to the ocean, but it's clear that there is a connection as the water rises and falls with the tides.

As far as locals are concerned, this blue hole is bottomless. No one's been able to prove that either. The salt water lake is brimming with tropical fish that you're free to feed or swim with, but fishing is not allowed.

Haunted House

Whether the ruins of the old Stewart Mansion on Harbour Island are haunted depends on who you ask. According to local legend, the family that resided there in grand style in the 1940s simply disappeared one night, leaving everything intact. A Greek shipping heir bought the mansion for his young bride in the 1960s, but after a half hour, she'd sensed something supernatural and vowed never to return. Twenty years later, fire gutted the once majestic homestead and all that remains is a shell.

134

Bat cave in Hatchet Bay

Queen's Highway, Hatchet Bay, Eleuthera. No admission fee.

If you didn't know these caves existed, you'd likely just keep on driving past. Watch for the rustic sign along the western side of the road near the big silos, drive along the dirt track and park in the first big clearing. You'll see the unmarked entrance to the cave. There is a ladder (it's only about 11ft down to the first landing) and stalactites and stalagmites cling to the ceiling and floor.

Venture in a little farther and you'll hear the bat colonies. They are harmless and there is no rabies in the Bahamas, but you will need a flashlight to catch a glimpse.

If, like many who came before, you feel compelled to etch your name on the interior walls of the caves, leave the marker and spray paint behind and instead use one of the chalky rocks lying on the cave floor.

Preacher's Cave in Eleuthera

North of The Bluff, Eleuthera. No admission fee.

Perhaps the most important historic sight on the island, Preacher's Cave is where it all began.

This is where the Eleutherian Adventurers, who gave the island its name, sought shelter after wrecking on a reef.

The new settlers held a religious service every year on the anniversary of the day they found safe refuge—a tradition that continued for 100 years.

They eventually ventured out and took up residence on nearby Spanish Wells and Harbour Island.

Preacher's Cave

© The Bahamas Ministry of Tourism

NATURAL SITES

WATERSPORTS

Eleuthera and Harbour Island are a scuba diver's dream destination. The best known dive spots vary in depth and features, so there's something different to experience every time you venture out. There are magnificent snorkeling reefs just offshore at almost every point.

Dive Sites

Current Cut

Current, Eleuthera.

This narrow channel separating Current Island from North Eleuthera creates one of the fastest **drift diving experiences** to be found. Fish (and divers) are swept at a rapid pace through the 2/3-mi long cut, and when the tide changes, they're pushed in the opposite direction. In addition to reef fish, expect to come face to face with sharks and rays as well. It usually takes just ten minutes to travel from end to end.

Devil's Backbone

Northern point of Eleuthera.

This spot on the way from Spanish Wells to Harbour Island has been the end of the road for many a captain for hundreds of years, so the wreck diving is impressive. The 292 foot long, 2,332 ton passenger steamship *Cienfuegos* sank after crashing into a reef in 1895. The wreckage lies scattered along the ocean floor. 200 yards east lies what's left of what researchers believe may have been one of Christopher Columbus' ships. All that's visible is a massive pile of ballast stones.

Train Wreck

Northern point of Eleuthera.

Actually part of the Devil's Backbone dive site, this feature is worthy of its own mention. More train wreck than shipwreck, it's what's left of a steam locomotive that sank in 1865 when it was being transported by wooden barge. Spot the wheels and boiler plate.

Scuba diving, Eleuthera

©The Bahamas Ministry of Tourism

Surf School

Bahamas Out Island Adventures, Harbour Island. 242-551-9635 or 242-335-0349. www.bahamas adventures.com. Contact for rates and to customize your tour. Group lessons from $60 per person.

Point breaks, reef breaks and beach breaks await you here. Learn to surf with the relaxed and friendly instructors taking you to the best spots and teaching you the skills. With at least four hours' surfing each day, they'll have you riding the waves in no time. They run three one-week courses each year, so book early. Bahamas Adventures also offer "surfaris", which are 1, 2 or 3 days and mix it up with snorkeling, kayaking, nighttime fun and beach time.

NIGHTLIFE

If you're looking for strong drinks, good music and dancing, Harbour Island's your best bet. But leave your fancy frock at home: These night-spots are very casual.

Gusty's

Coconut Grove Avenue, Harbour Island. 242-333-2165. No admission fee. Gets going around 11pm and closes at 1am.

Park your golf cart outside, take off your shoes and hit the sandy dance floor at this staple on the Briland night scene.
The decor is graffiti-covered walls, a long wooden bar, and a wraparound porch where you can catch the breeze in between dance numbers.
There's usually a DJ playing, but every so often you'll find a live band playing local music.
Locals and tourists usually get the night started here.

Seagrapes

Colebrook Street, Harbour Island. No admission fee. Gets going around 11pm and stays open late.

If it weren't for the loud music pulsing from within, you'd never guess this to be a nightclub. It's simple, but popular with the locals.

Vic-Hum

Barrack & Munnings Street, Harbour Island. 242-333-2161. No admission fee. Opens late, and stays open late.

To say this little joint is unusual is an understatement. It looks tiny from the outside, but keeps going and going once you get in the door.
There's a pool table and most nights speakers blast old school and current reggae tunes.
It can get a little rowdy inside and in front of the entrance, but the crowd is harmless and friendly. The dance floor doubles as a basketball court by day.
Make sure you check out the world's largest coconut before heading home. It's behind the bar.

THE EXUMAS: GREAT EXUMA, LITTLE EXUMA, EXUMA CAYS★★

These islands are known for natural beauty, incredible aquamarine waters, bird and marine life. 365 cays, some of which disappear at high tide, run 100 miles from north to south.

Great Exuma & Little Exuma

Great Exuma dwarfs the other islands that make up the Exuma chain.

It's home to most of the chain's 3,500 residents and is where you'll find the island's main settlement of **George Town** and a smattering of other villages that date back to the island's slavery past.

George Town is the island's economic and administrative center, and is built around the small Lake Victoria. Just a few miles north of the town center is the Exuma international airport.

North and south of George Town are other small settlements with little more than a few homes, some plantation ruins, and perhaps a schoolhouse.

Little Exuma has the remains of a cotton plantation dating back to the 1700s and some gorgeous tranquil beaches. It is joined to its larger neighbor by a small bridge running over a creek.

The Exuma Cays★★

There's a different cay to explore for every day of the year in the Exuma chain, and each is beautiful in its own right.

For years yachtsmen have been heading down the cays, delighting in their natural pristine beauty. From the sky, the tiny cays look like a necklace strung together.

Most of the cays are uninhabited, some are privately owned. Movie star Johnny Depp and country music stars Faith Hill and Tim Mcgraw have their own islands. In the Bahamas, all beaches are public up to the high water mark, so you're free to go exploring so long as you have a small boat.

Kidd's Cove, George Town, Great Exuma

©The Bahamas Ministry of Tourism

RESORTS

Whether you're looking for a tiny family run guesthouse, a trendy boutique resort, or one of the most expensive places to lay your head in the Bahamas, Exuma and its Cays have lots to choose from. For more information and to find hotels not part of major resorts see *Must Stay*.

$$$$$	over $650	$$	$100–$250
$$$$	$400–$650	$	under $100
$$$	$250–$400		

Musha Cay and the Islands of Copperfield Bay

$$$$$ 12 rooms
Exuma Cays. 203-602-0300 or 877-889-1100. www.mushacay.com.

There are 365 cays in the Exuma chain; book a night for $32,250 plus tax and 11 of them are all yours.

Pick from any of the five guesthouses, one of them a sprawling 10,000sq ft two-bedroom house with commanding 360 degree views of the entire property.

For the exorbitant price tag, you can bring along up to 11 other people, use all 5 houses, get exclusive use of 40 beaches including the legendary 2mi-long sand bar, four boats ranging from 22–37ft jet skis, 28ft catamaran, non-motorized water sport equipment, outdoor movie theater, state of the art fitness center, championship tennis court, jogging paths and adventure trails, and even Houdini's personal billiard table. All meals and beverages at the Balinese Beach Pavillion and The Landings Restaurant are also included in the rate.

If you want to go on a treasure hunt designed by property owner magician David Copperfield, you'll have to pay extra.

Four Seasons Great Exuma at Emerald Bay

$$$ 180 rooms
Queen's Highway, Emerald Bay, Great Exuma. 242-336-6800. www.fourseasons.com/greatexuma.

Four Seasons put Great Exuma on the map with the in-crowd. It's the first and only international resort brand found anywhere in the chain of islands.

The idyllic setting lends itself to the kind of romance and relaxation Four Seasons is known for. There's a Greg Norman-designed championship golf course and a spa—the only ones you'll find on the island, and the restaurants here take island dining to a whole other level. Rooms and suites are sophisticated yet still fit their island setting. The full service spa has 19 treatment rooms and an open-air spa garden.

Club Peace and Plenty

$$ 32 rooms
Queen's Highway, George Town, Great Exuma. 242-336-2551 or 1-800-525-2210. www.peaceandplenty.com.

Exuma's oldest hotel still commands a crowd. Locals and guests gather at the hotel bar nightly for drinks and special theme nights. The main house was originally a

139

sponge warehouse and then a family home. It was converted into a hotel in the 1940s.

Rooms have views of lovely Elizabeth Harbour, the resort garden and its small pool. You can easily wander into George Town from the Club.

Staniel Cay Yacht Club

$$ 13 rooms
Staniel Cay, Exuma Cays. 242-355-2024. www.stanielcay.com.

Staniel Cay equals tranquillity. This 2sq mi island just north of Great Exuma has a small village and the Staniel Cay Yacht Club, which has been an integral part of the community since 1956.

Guests stay in one of the 9 one and two-bedroom pastel cottages overlooking the water. They're designed and equipped to be a true home away from home. Rooms are void of televisions, telephone and internet, but all those creature comforts are available at the clubhouse.

There are no ATMs on Staniel Cay and the resort is just about the only place to accept credit cards.

St Francis Resort

$$ 8 rooms
Stocking Island, Exuma. 242-557-9629. www.stfrancisresort.com.

Perched on a hilltop on Stocking Island, just a few minutes by boat from the mainland, the villas at St Francis Resort have incredible views of both the harbor and the Atlantic Ocean. Rooms have deep balconies and right outside is a private 5mi-long beach.

Aerial view of Staniel Cay Yacht Club

© The Bahamas Ministry of Tourism

BEACHES

Exuma and its cays are known for having some of the most amazing beaches anywhere in the world. With a tiny population on the mainland, and no one on most of the cays, privacy is guaranteed. Drive along the mainland and stop off wherever a stretch of sand catches your fancy, or rent a boat for an unforgettable day of cay hopping.

Beaches of Great Exuma

Rent a car and drive north or south of George Town to find some of the most incredible, unspoiled beaches you've ever seen.
Coco Plum Beach and Three Sisters Beach are lovely northern beaches. Head south to little Exuma for great snorkeling at the Tropic of Cancer Beach, also called Pelican Beach by locals.

Saddle Cay Beach

Saddle Cay, Exuma Cays.

The shape of this little island makes it stand out from the rest of the cays. The horseshoe formation

Chat 'n' Chill Bar and beach, Stocking Island

has created a spectacular, untouched white sand beach. You'll need a boat to get here.

Stocking Island

Across Elizabeth Harbour from George Town. 242-336-2700.

Just a few minutes across Elizabeth Harbour from George Town, Stocking Island is one of the hottest spots in the islands.
Hundreds of boats of every size, and even the occasional seaplane, pull up to the picturesque cove every Sunday. The draw? Besides the beautiful beach and shallow aquamarine waters, it's where you'll find **Chat 'n' Chill**. This rustic bar, restaurant and beach playground was created in 1998 by Exumian 'banker turned beach bum' Kenneth Bowe. On Sundays, the action gets going with 'beach church' at 10am followed by an all day **pig roast**.
Down by the ocean there's always a line of people at the conch shack, patiently waiting on fresh-made conch salad.

Coco Plum Beach

Queen's Highway, Emerald Bay, Great Exuma.

If you're hoping to take home some beautiful shells, head to this sandy stretch just next to the Four Seasons Resort. As the tide rolls out, a treasure trove of shells and sand dollars is left behind.

Tropic of Cancer Beach

Little Exuma.

The drive down to Little Exuma is worth doing, especially if you're on the hunt for one of the most beautiful beaches in the island chain. Tropic of Cancer Beach, called Pelican Beach by the locals, is a fantastic snorkeling spot, and there's a hut with benches so you can escape the beating sun for a few minutes while enjoying the natural beauty. You'll know you've arrived when you see the name "Tropic of Cancer" carved into the concrete ramp leading down to the beach.

BEACHES

NATURAL SITES

With such unspoiled beauty, it's no surprise that Exuma and the Cays have long been a haven for wildlife both in and out of the water. You'll need to get in a boat to see some of the most amazing natural sites.

The Exuma Cays Land and Sea Park★★

North Exuma Cays.

Created in 1958, the Exuma Land and Sea Park was ahead of its time. What makes it truly unique is that a number of privately owned cays fall within the protected area. The 112,640 acre land and sea park includes Little Wax Cay, Shroud Cay, Little Pigeon Cay, Hawksbill Cay, Little Hawksbill Cay, Cistern Cay, Long Cay, Warderick Wells, Halls Pond Cay, Little White Bay Cay, South Halls Pond Cay, Soldier Cay, O'Brien's/Pasture Cays, Bell Island, Little Bell Island and Rocky Dundas.

The park has a diverse ecosystem and in 1985, was declared an absolute no take zone. You're not even allowed to take a shell off one of the beaches, much less go fishing. The only land mammal native to the Bahamas, the Hutia, lives within the park, as do iguanas,

marine life and sea birds.
The park's headquarters is located on Warderick Wells island. On this island, as well as on Hawksbill Cay and Hall's Pond, you can find marked nature trails.

Allan's Cay

Top of the Exuma Cays.

This small island near the top of the Exuma chain is home to hundreds of **endangered iguanas**.

They look vicious, but are actually a very gentle lizard. The Allan's Cay iguanas are used to human interaction and dash out of the seagrape tree and coco plum bush shade toward the water as soon as they hear a boat approaching. These dragon-like amphibians are happy to have visitors, especially when they're presented with grapes skewered on the end of sticks.

Aerial view of the Exuma Cays Land and Sea Park

© The Bahamas Ministry of Tourism

Rolleville & Rolle Town

Get to know some of the friendly locals while staying in Exuma and you may start to notice that just about all of them have the last name 'Rolle'.
Their ancestors were likely slaves owned by Englishman Lord John Rolle.
It was common practice for African slaves to adopt the last name of their owner. Rolle owned five cotton plantations across the island. Emancipation came, and rather than just let his slaves go, Rolle, whose cotton business was failing, apparently left his land to his slaves.
Rolleville in the north and Rolle Town to the south, are two of about five settlements formed around the old Rolle plantations and are home to hundreds of Rolles to this day. No documentation of the master's deed has ever been found, and much of the land remains undeveloped because none of the modern day Rolles can gain clear title. *Rolleville – 28mi north of George Town; Rolle Town – 5mi south of George Town.*

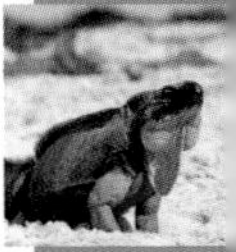

Lake Victoria

George Town, Great Exuma.

George Town is actually built around the perimeter of this small lake, joined to Elizabeth Harbour by a narrow passage.
It was named after Queen Victoria, and although it's not all that much to look at now, it used to have phosphorous elements making it glow on windy nights.

Norman's Cay

Top of the Exuma Cays.

One of the northernmost cays in the Exuma chain, Norman's Cay has a particularly colorful history. Colombian drug lord Carlos Lehder took up residence in the early-1980s, and ran his illicit trade from the island. Millions of dollars' worth of cocaine is believed to have come in and out of this unlikely distribution point.
To help things along, Lehder built a 3,300ft runway, and had armed guards and attack dogs patrolling the coast.
The local government eventually began to crack down on Lehder and confiscated his property. Lehder fled and was arrested in the United States, and Norman's Cay has stood still in time.

Three Sisters Rocks

Mount Thompson, Great Exuma.

As the legend goes, once upon a time in Exuma there were three sisters who had the misfortune to fall in love with one man. When they discovered this handsome young Englishman had captured all of their hearts, they took him out to sea and drowned him and themselves, putting the sisters out of their misery. According to local lore, the three rocks then sprung up from the ocean.

OUTDOOR SPORTS

It was only with the opening of the Four Seasons that the traditional vacation land-based activities were added to what Exuma has to offer.

Golf

Four Seasons, Queen's Highway, Emerald Bay, Great Exuma. 242-336-6800. www.fourseasons. com/greatexuma. Tee times 7am–4pm daily.

Golf legend Greg Norman was brought on board to design this championship 18-hole course. Situated on a private peninsula, there are six signature holes hugging the coast. It's hard to stay focused on your game as you watch the turquoise ocean change its hue.

The par 72 course is environmentally friendly, using seashore paspalum grass. There's a pro shop with everything you need.

Tennis

Four Seasons, Queen's Highway, Emerald Bay, Great Exuma. 242-336-6800. www.fourseasons. com/greatexuma.

The team behind the Four Seasons realized it would be hard to pull vacationers away from the beach during the day, so they outfitted the resort with six Hydro Har-Tru courts that are all lit for night play. The pro shop has all you need for rent or sale, and the resort tennis pros offer a range of programs and lessons to help you improve your game.

WATERSPORTS

You're probably going to spend most of your Exuma vacation in or on the water; as you're flying in, you'll begin to understand why. Exuma boasts some of the most beautiful aquamarine waters in the Bahamas.

Dive Sites

Thunderball Grotto★★

Made famous in James Bond flicks *Never Say Never Again* and *Thunderball* for which it was named, as well Disney's *Splash*, this exceptional dive site (you can snorkel, too, at low tide) is just northwest of Staniel Cay.

It's actually a hollowed-out island teeming with colorful fish, coral heads and an array of sponges.

Amberjack Reef

Caribbean Reef and nurse sharks hang out on this 50ft patch reef. Dive operators make excursions there for shark feeding dives but there are lots of other interesting sea creatures including eels and of course, hundreds of jacks.

Mysterious Cave

Jacques Cousteau discovered and explored this unusual underwater tunnel found just off Stocking Is-

Regatta Time

Sailing regattas are a favorite pastime throughout the islands of the Bahamas. The National Family Island Regatta held in George Town's Elizabeth Harbour is the grand daddy of Bahamian sailing. Every April since the mid-1950s, sloops, dinghies and yachts gather for three days of intense competition testing skill and endurance. Only Bahamian made and owned sailboats are allowed to compete. Onshore, it's party time. Most of the revelers, and there are thousands who flock to the island at regatta time, are oblivious to what's going on in the harbor.

land. The dive runs 400ft deep and shouldn't be attempted without an experienced guide.

Kayaking

Starfish Adventure Center. Queen's Highway, George Town, Great Exuma. 1-877-398-6222. www. exuma-bahamas.com/starfish.

The calm, shallow waters surrounding the **Exuma Cays★★** are ideal for exploring by kayak. Starfish offers fun-filled day and week-long kayaking excursions that let you explore the beauty of nearby cays from a completely different perspective.
Tours and rentals include basic kayaking instruction.
If you prefer to head out on your own, you can rent kayaks by the hour, day or week from Starfish or from many of the island hotels.

Motor and Sail Boat Rentals

Motorboats—*Minns Water Sports. George Town, Great Exuma. 242-336-3483.*

The best way to truly experience Exuma is by boat. Minns has 15ft–22ft boats for rent. Prices range from $120 to $260 for a

single day or $90 to $210 per day if you're renting for a week.

Sailboats—*Starfish Adventure. Queen's Highway, George Town, Great Exuma. 1-877-398-6222. www.exuma-bahamas.com/ starfish Center.*

Starfish rents out hobie wave and sea pearls by the hour or by the day or week. Prices, which include life jackets and a chart, range from $50 for two hours to $525 for the week on a Hobie wave. The sea pearl is only available for a full day or week ($200 and $995). Weekly rentals also come with dry bags, bailer and a cooler.

Swim with Dolphins or Pigs

Pods of wild bottlenose dolphins love the crystal-clear waters of the **Exuma Cays★★** as much as the yachting crowd does, so it's not uncommon to find yourself swimming alongside a few offshore. For something a little more out of the ordinary, head over to Major's Cay, not far from Staniel Cay. Here, you'll find a group of swimming pigs who call the cay home. They're harmless, and would love you to bring them a treat for lunch.

SOUTH ISLANDS

The farther south you travel the fewer people you'll see. Settlements on the southern islands are barely populated, and tourism facilities are rustic for the most part, but the natural beauty is breathtaking.

Acklins Island

Just over 400 people and many, many iguanas call this remote undeveloped island home. It's just 92sq mi and there's no tourism offerings to speak of. But if you're looking for solitude in a rugged natural setting, this is the place to go. Serious bonefish and big game fishermen flock to Acklins for the very reasons others stay away.

Cat Island

Home to the country's highest natural point—206 foot high Mount Alvernia, Cat Island is one of the most interesting islands culturally. With more effort being put into the tourism infrastructure, Cat Island has recently been emerging as a favorite off the beaten path Bahamas vacation destination. With nature trails at every turn, some of the best dive and snorkel sites in the country, ruins of old cotton plantations and a little talked about reputation for

obeah (black magic), there's lots to see and do. The African-Bahamian culture is a fascinating aspect to Cat Island, myths and folklore live on in the ancestors of African Slaves. Cat Island's most famous son of the soil is Hollywood star, Sir Sidney Poitier.

Crooked Island

It's hard to imagine it today, but just over a hundred years ago, Crooked Island was a bustling boom town. At the turn of the 19th century there were as many as 50 cotton plantations, but by 1820, the cotton industry had failed and the island's boom was over. So important was this island, that the country's first general post office was located at Landrail Point.

Inagua

According to a local rake 'n' scrape song, "Inagua is the best kept secret in the Bahamas." That could

Ruins of a plantation on Cat Island

MUST SEE   SOUTH ISLANDS

be because it's closer to Cuba than Nassau.

Inagua is a true company town. The island is intrinsically linked to the Morton Salt Company's salt mining facility in.

The third largest island in the Bahamas is home to a colony of more than 60,000 flamingos. They outnumber human beings there 60 to one.

More than 50 percent of the island's mass is included in a protected **National Park★★**.

Long Island

Long Island is the most developed of the southern islands, but that's not saying much. In fact, it has only been the past 15 years that the Island has had electricity. Eighty miles of uninterrupted coast gives this island its name. The landscape is diverse and the views are breathtaking. From swamps to lush and green rolling hills, to white sand beaches and plunging cliffs, Long Island is incredibly picturesque. There are many secluded caves inland and Long Island also boasts the deepest underwater cavern in the Bahamas: **Dean's Blue Hole★★**. There is considerable archeological evidence that the Lucayan Tainos once lived here and it is generally agreed that Columbus stopped here in 1492. In the 1800s, the Loyalists moved in, setting up cotton plantations and sheep and cattle farms. With the end of slavery in 1834 came the end of this era. Plantation ruins make for interesting exploration.

Today, most employment comes from fishing and construction. The small central hub is Salt Pond, where you can buy provisions.

© The Bahamas Ministry of Tourism

Exploring Long Island

San Salvador

The small island is the outermost of the Bahamas and is where Christopher Columbus reportedly discovered the New World on October 12, 1492.

It's actually the peak of a mountain that sinks 15,000ft down to the ocean floor. Just about 1,000 people call this 12 by 5mi island home and they take laid back living to a whole new level.

A top-notch Club Med makes it a more popular destination than it might otherwise be for anyone not into rugged exploration and solitary days on white sand beaches. Aside from lazing on picturesque beaches, visitors spend their time diving, snorkeling and fishing. Birdlife is also a big draw here. Cockburn (pronounced co-burn) is the main center on the island, and the dilapidated Queen's Highway runs through here on its route of the outskirts of the island. In fact, most of the interior of the island is underwater, so locals get around by boat.

RESORTS

Resorts in the southern islands of the Bahama chain tend to be quite basic and have a definite 'island feel'. Most of them place great emphasis on ways to help you enjoy the water, and usually have all the amenities you need, as the towns aren't set up to cater to tourists. For more information and to find hotels not part of major resorts see *Must Stay*.

$$$$$	over $650	**$$**	$100–$250
$$$$	$400–$650	**$**	under $100
$$$	$250–$400		

Cape Santa Maria Beach Resort

© The Bahamas Ministry of Tourism

🐚 Cape Santa Maria Beach Resort and Villas

$$$ **44 rooms**
Stella Maris, Long Island.
242-338-5273 or 1-800-663-7090.
www.capesantamaria.com.

The condo-style villas at this boutique beachfront resort are, in a word, stunning.

Once you've experienced the large windows and balconies overlooking one of the most amazing beaches you've ever laid eyes on, soaked in the jetted tub, hung out in the beautiful appointed open plan living and kitchen area, you're never going to want to go home. The smaller bungalows that open right onto the beach are equally appealing.

Cape Santa Maria is on the northwest coast of Long Island, just over a ten-minute taxi ride from Stella Maris airport, or a 50 minutes drive from Deadman's Cay airport. The 4mi-long powdery white sand beach and shallow aquamarine water are a beach lover's paradise.

Club Med

$$$ **264 rooms**
North of Riding Rock, San Salvador.
242-331-2000 or 1-888-932-2582.
www.clubmed.com.

If Christopher Columbus had stumbled across this Club Med property when he discovered the New World, chances are he'd never have left San Salvador. All-inclusive as all Club Med properties are, this one has an air of elegance and upscale luxuriance.

Bungalows are scattered along this bougainvillea-covered property

© Club Med

Massage on the beach, Club Med

Fernandez Bay Village

and many have views of the tranquil Bonefish Bay. All rooms have either an outside patio or a balcony. At the three restaurants you can choose from Bahamian to Brazilian cuisine. Three bars keep the party going until 2am.

A range of activities—from aquafitness in the pool to skiing and wakeboarding in the bay—is included in your package, and in case you aren't relaxed enough, for an extra charge you can book a massage package.

Crooked Island Lodge

$$ 12 rooms
Pittstown Point Landings, Crooked Island. 242-344-2507. www.pittstownpoint.com.

There's nothing particularly fancy about this motel-style beachfront lodge, but its surroundings are so incredible you're not going to be bothered.

Formerly the Pittstown Point Landings, this rustic resort has long been top of the list for fishing fanatics. Whether you're looking for bonefishing in the flats or deep sea fishing for bigger game, you'll be perfectly situated.

There's a decent restaurant on property—a bonus considering there's not much more on offer on the island.

The lodge also has its own 2,000 foot runway so you can fly right in.

Fernandez Bay Village

$$ 18 rooms
New Bight, Cat Island. 242-342-2018. www.fernandez bayvillage.com.

Two-person villas with secluded patios and outdoor garden baths help make this boutique resort special. The private, mile-long white sand beach, perfect for romantic strolls and cooling dips in the sea, is an added attraction. Cottages and villas dot the landscape. The cottages sleep two, while the more spacious villas are designed to accommodate four to six people comfortably. There's usually a nice breeze blowing, but if air conditioning is a must, make sure you say so when booking as not all rooms are equipped. Several villas have full kitchens, and there is a nearby market and grocery store to buy provisions from. However, there is also an

RESORTS

Hawk's Nest Resort and Marina

© The Bahamas Ministry of Tourism

excellent restaurant serving breakfast, lunch and dinner on property if you're taking a vacation from cooking.

Hawk's Nest Resort and Marina

$$ 12 rooms
Devil's Point, Cat Island. 242-342-7050. www.hawks-nest.com.

Hawk's Nest has the best marina facilities in the south, making it a favorite with boaters.
Its recently upgraded beachfront rooms and four-star service make it a favorite with land lubbers, too. It's situated at Cat Island's southern tip has its own recently resurfaced 3,100ft-long private airstrip just a few hundred feet from the resort. There's a fully equipped PADI dive center, elegant restaurant overlooking the sea, and two bars.

Sammy T's

$$ 8 rooms
Bennet's Harbour, Cat Island. 242-354-6009 or 242-427-5897. www.sammytbahamas.com.

You'll find the intimate Sammy T's tucked into a protected cove with

an absolutely spectacular pink sand beach. It's the creation of Cat Island native Sammy T, who had a hand in every detail. Guests stay in wooden villas that look weather beaten but have only been there since 2003. Inside, there's tile flooring, air conditioning, rattan furniture and a kitchenette with microwave and fridge. No children under 10 years old means the peaceful ambience is never broken.

Pigeon Cay Beach Club

$ 8 rooms
Pigeon Cay, Cat Island. 242-354-5084. www.pigeoncay-bahamas.com.

Three miles of private white sand beach and only seven cottages means you're guaranteed a private place to set up your lounge chair at Pigeon Cay. It's located on a northern ridge overlooking an 8mi-long bay.
Cottages aren't air conditioned, but they're just steps away from the beach, so the ocean breeze will keep you cool.
Bahamian-style continental breakfast is included and you whip

up a meal yourself or order lunch or dinner in the restaurant or in your room. There's a bar, which operates on an honor system so you'll get chance to practice your bartending skills.

At Pigeon Cay you'll truly escape the outside world—there's no phone, television or internet.

Riding Rock Inn

$ **42 rooms**
Riding Rock, San Salvador.
242-331-2631 or 1-800-272-1492.
www.ridingrock.com.

For those San Salvador visitors looking for something a little more rustic and island authentic, family-owned Riding Rock Inn is ideal. Air-conditioned rooms are basic, but all have televisions, phones, and a mini fridge.

There's a full service marina and scuba dive center; just offshore are some of the island's best dive and snorkel sites. For a more relaxing day, lounge on the beach or by the freshwater swimming pool.

A restaurant serves three meals daily. Fresh fish for dinner is always a favorite here.

Stella Maris Resort

$ **21 rooms**
Stella Maris, Long Island.
242-338-2051/2/3 or 1-800-426-
0466. www.stellamarisresort.com.

You've got three freshwater swimming pools and seven private beaches to choose from when you stay at this hilltop resort.

If that's not enough, book one of the houses with its own private infinity pool.

Accommodations run the gamut from simple but spacious rooms in the two-story hotel to fully appointed four-bedroom, two-bathroom houses with their own pool. Regardless of the room you select, you'll have a great view.

A full slate of free, optional activities day and night guarantee you'll never get bored.

The resort offers free twice-daily excursions, boat cruises twice a week, and all the equipment you'll need for your own adventure by land or sea.

At night, there's everything from live rake 'n' scrape music to nature slide shows and history talks.

Stella Maris Resort Club

RESORTS

BEACHES

What the southern islands of the Bahamas lack in modern facilities and attractions, they make up for in beaches. You could spend your entire vacation exploring some of the most beautiful beaches in the world. Some are picture-postcard perfect, while others are great for shelling, and still others are little-known surfing spots.

Cape Santa Maria Beach, Long Island

© The Bahamas Ministry of Tourism

Cape Santa Maria Beach★★

Stella Maris, Long Island.

This is quite possibly the best beach in the entire Bahamas. Time and again it's made lists of the top ten beaches found anywhere in the world.
Four uninterrupted miles of powder-white sand, swaying palm trees providing shade from the scorching sun, and shallow sea in every possible shade of blue make this beach pure perfection.

Love Beach★

Stella Maris, Long Island.

This romantically named beach on the northeastern coast is actually a string of perfect beaches, each about a half mile long. Love Beach proper is a wonderful place to take

kids as the limestone rocks create a natural swimming pool that's completely protected from the elements.

Bathing Beach, Shell Beach & French Wells

Landrail Point, Crooked Island.

There's not an awful lot to see and do in Crooked Island, but if beaches are your thing, you've found the right place. These three breathtaking beaches roll into one another along a spectacular 7mi-long stretch. There's great snorkeling on reefs just offshore in the Crooked Island Passage, and these beaches are almost always guaranteed to be completely deserted until you show up.

Deal's Beach

Northwestern coast of Long Island.

On the opposite coast to the Love Beaches, this roadside beach is the perfect place to stop off for lunch. With trees for shade, a built-in barbecue grill and tables and benches, all you need to bring is the picnic.

East Beach

United Estates, San Salvador.

Three miles of pure rose-pink sand on the northeast coast. You're likely to be the only person here no matter what time of day you arrive. This is a fantastic place for snorkeling, although there has been talk of sharks spotted here, so check with islanders first.

Fountain Bay Beach

New Bight, Cat Island.

This off-the-beaten-path beach near Bridge Inn gets its name from an in-ground, natural fountain. Venture into the bushes near the bonefish flats and you'll be sure to find it. The beach itself is a good mile long and there are wonderful snorkeling reefs right offshore.

French Bay

Southeastern coast of San Salvador.

Surfers who have stumbled upon this beach have cursed themselves for not bringing their boards with them.
Don't go here expecting the typical white sand beach. The shore here is sharp limestone. The ocean offshore is rough, so experienced surfers will find it thrilling. Beyond the crashing waves lies an extensive reef system.

Sandy Point

6mi south of Cockburn Town, San Salvador.

It takes a bit of effort to get to this southern point, but there's lots to see and do, so it's worth the effort. Sandy Point Beach is a pretty, wide stretch of sand. Nearby is Grotto Bay, a favorite snorkeling spot. While in the area, be sure to plan time for a visit to the ruins of Watlings Castle *(see p 155)*.

Typical pink sand beach on Cat Island

© The Bahamas Ministry of Tourism

BEACHES

HISTORIC BUILDINGS AND MUSEUMS

In the 18th century Loyalists fled America and established plantations on the Southern Islands. The emancipation of slaves and unsuitable soil meant they were not successful ventures. There are few existing memorials to the region's importance in days gone by and, unfortunately, many of the historic buildings are in ruins.

SOUTH ISLANDS

Mount Alvernia Hermitage★

New Bight, Cat Island. No admission fee. See Mount Alvernia p 157.

Father Jerome was an Anglican priest who converted to Catholicism. All together, he built four beautiful churches across the Bahamas. However, his most famous legacy is The Hermitage high atop Mount Alvernia.

The Englishman, born John Hawes, was an award-winning architect before he turned to the priesthood. The bell tower, chapel and other buildings are built of bricks he carved out of limestone by hand. Father Jerome, who was considered a saint by locals, died in Cat Island in 1956 at the age of 80.

Farquharson Plantation

Southeast Coast, San Salvador. No admission fee.

These are considered some of the best preserved plantation ruins in the Bahamas. Some refer to it as "Blackbeard's Castle" because the infamous pirate is known to have frequented the area. The buildings include what might have been a great house, a prison and a kitchen. There is also a cattle trough cut out of solid rock.

New World Museum

Palmetto Grove, Cockburn Town, San Salvador. By appointment. 242-323-3182. No admission fee.

The debate over just where Christopher Columbus first discovered

Hermitage, Cat Island

©The Bahamas Ministry of Tourism

MUST SEE

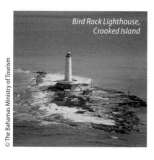

*Bird Rock Lighthouse,
Crooked Island*

Bird Rock Lighthouse

*Crooked Island Passage,
Crooked Island.*

This white lighthouse is 115ft high and still guides boat captains through the challenging cut into the island.

Dixon Hill Lighthouse

*United Estates, San Salvador.
Leave a dollar when you sign
the guest book.*

The **views**★ from the top of the lighthouse will take your breath away—quite literally. It's a 160-foot climb. The lighthouse was built on an old plantation in 1887 and to this day is hand cranked. The lighthouse keeper is always on duty.

Great Inagua Lighthouse

Matthew Town, Inagua.

This white lighthouse built in 1870 gives off two white flashes every ten seconds and can be seen from 19.2mi away.

Watling's Castle Ruins

*Sandy Point, San Salvador.
No admission fee.*

Pirates made it down this far south in the 18th century. Watling's Castle is what's left of a late-18th century Loyalist plantation house. The ruins were named after an English Buccaneer who went by the names John and George Watling. In fact, until 1925, San Salvador was officially called Watling's Island.
Today, the ruins include the three-story great house, an outdoor kitchen, slave quarters and buildings once used for storage.

the New World rages on. But San Salvador residents feel there's nothing to discuss and pay homage to the fateful landing in 1492. The tiny New World Museum contains artifacts from an original Arawak Indian settlement, Lucayan pottery and paintings of Columbus' landfall. The building it's housed in was constructed in 1910 and used to be the island's jail.

Southern Island Lighthouses

There are just three kerosene-lit lighthouses left in the world, all of them in the Bahamas.
These navigational guides were put up mostly by the Imperial Lighthouse Service back in the days when the southern Bahamas was a hub of activity on the high seas. A halfway point between North and South America, the southern Bahamas was a transshipment location for goods. To this day, most of the remaining lighthouses serve a critical navigational role.

PARKS AND GARDENS

With so few people, the islands of the southern Bahamas provide some of the most amazing unspoiled, natural sites. The Bahamas National Trust is a key player to ensure these areas continue to survive.

Inagua National Park★★

Matthew Town, Inagua. Phone to arrange a visit 242-393-1317. www.bnt.bs/parks.php.

The crown in the Bahamas National Trust's collection of protected parks, Inagua's National Park is a sanctuary for wildlife.
Occupying more than half of the island's mass, the park is best known for its colony of West Indian flamingos and is actually credited with bringing these beautiful creatures back from near extinction. Today, there are between 60,000 and 80,000 living in the park.

Pink Flamingos

Inagua is home to the largest breeding colony of West Indian Flamingos in the world. They've thrived feeding off the brine found in the salt flats operated by the Morton Salt Company. It's their salty diet that turns their feathers such a rich, vibrant pink.

Bird watchers willing to get up before dawn will also see other exotic birds including Bahama parrots, pelicans, herons, egrets, and Bahama pintail ducks, brown pelicans, tri-colored herons, snowy egrets, reddish egrets, stripe-headed tanangers, cormorants, roseate spoonbills, American kestrels, and burrowing owls
It has been declared an "important bird area" by Birdlife International. Inagua's wild donkeys are also thriving in the protected park which includes Lake Rosa, the largest lake in the Bahamas.

Hope Great House

Crooked Island

Once the focal point of a 19th century plantation, Hope Great House is now in ruins. Over the years, nature took over, creating some beautiful, wild gardens. The Bahamas National Trust took over the spot and it's now a protected area.

Flamingos on Great Inagua

© Bob Krist/Corbis

NATURAL SITES

The islands in the southern Bahamas have a fascinating history and there are also some incredible natural marvels to see. Apart from Long Island, they aren't really touched by tourism, so you may have to ask around for a local guide.

Dean's Blue Hole, Long Island.

© The Bahamas Ministry of Tourism

Dean's Blue Hole★★

Turtle Cove, Long Island.

This massive blue hole is said to be 663ft deep, but Long Islanders swear it's bottomless.

In any event, even if the measured depth holds true, Dean's Blue Hole holds the honor of being the world's second-largest underwater cavern.

It measures roughly 120ft across at the surface and is surrounded by rocky limestone cliffs on three sides and a powder white beach on the fourth. You can take a swim with fish and turtles in the persistently calm water.

Mount Alvernia

New Bight, Cat Island. See Mount Alvernia Hermitage p 154.

Only in the Bahamas do they have the audacity to call a bump that rises 206ft above sea level "Mount" anything. The highest natural point in the entire Bahamas was originally called Como Hill, but

Father Jerome, who lived atop the peak in his Hermitage *(see p 154)*, renamed it in honor of the Tuscan site where Saint Francis received the wounds of the cross.

Leading up the mountainside are the 12 Stations of the Cross, painstakingly carved by Father Jerome. High atop Mount Alvernia are stunning panoramic views of the island as well as the tomb where Father Jerome is buried. He is said to have been buried barefoot without a casket.

Hamilton's Cave

Petty's, Long Island.

One of the largest documented caves in the Bahamas at 1,500ft deep, Hamilton's Cave still has Lucayan artifacts inside and ancient paintings on the walls. This part freshwater, part saltwater cave is lined with stalactites and stalagmites. The way to remember the difference—stalactites cling 'tite' to the ceiling and stalagmites 'mite' grow up to reach them.

HISTORIC SITES

The Southern Islands first hit the map when Christopher Columbus set sail in search of the New World and landed on San Salvador. At least that's the prevailing theory. Over time, the indigenous Lucayans were cold bloodedly wiped out by their contact with Europeans.

SOUTH ISLANDS

MUST SEE

Cartwright's Cave

Mortimer's, Long Island.
No admission fee.

This cave is so far off the beaten track that it's not likely you'll be able to find it without a local guide.
In 1988, local man Carlton Cartwright discovered three duhos—the ceremonial stools used by the Lucayan Indians who once inhabited the area.
For tours, call Leonard Cartwright (242-337-0235).

Columbus Cove

Stella Maris, Long Island.

Long Island is the third island in the Bahama chain that Christopher Columbus sailed to.
To commemorate this historic event, Long Islanders have erected a small monument and plaque. The road that leads up to the 15ft concrete and iron monument is rocky, but the views are incredible and it's neat to stand there and think that five hundred years ago, Columbus did the same thing.

Columbus Landing Cross

Long Bay, San Salvador.

Some believe Columbus actually first landed on Samana Cay, just off the coast of Crooked Island, but until someone comes along with hard evidence to the contrary, San Salvador holds onto the title. Propped on the beach he and his crew are believed to have first come ashore, is a simple white cross erected on Christmas Day, 1956. The ten-acre area around the cross is a rich archeological site.

Chicago Herald Monument

East Beach, San Salvador.

This is one time the press truly got it wrong. In June 1891, in advance of the World's Fair to be held in Chicago in 1893, *The Chicago Herald* erected a monument to mark Columbus' landfall in San Salvador. Only thing is, they put it at the wrong spot. The landfall actually happened on the opposite side of the island!

It's All in a Name

The names of settlements dotting the southern Bahamas are as colorful as the people who live there. Long Islander's have some unfortunate sounding addresses, including Deadman's Cay, Burnt Ground and Hard Bargain.
The towns in Acklins and Crooked Island—Snug Corner, Delectable Bay and Spring Point—sound much more inviting.

WATERSPORTS

The snorkeling and diving in the southern Bahamas is phenomenal. Good thing, because there's not a whole lot else to do. Whether you're looking for a shallow reef to swim around or want to venture into a mysterious blue hole, you'll have your pick of sites.

Dive Sites

Dean's Blue Hole★★

Turtle Cove, Long Island.

Officially, Dean's Blue Hole bottoms out at 663ft. It's the second-largest underwater cavern system in the world and although it's well inland, the fish, turtles and rays that swim around are evidence that it's connected to the ocean at some point.

Shark Reef

Stella Maris, Long Island.

The first shark dive established in the Bahamas, most agree it's still the best. Gray-tipped reef sharks, bull sharks and nurse sharks come out to greet divers, as does the occasional hammerhead. Guides feed the sharks while divers hover in a circle around the action. It's about 30ft deep and takes about a half hour to get there by boat.

Doolittle's Grotto

Southwestern San Salvador.

Caves and grottos abound at this site and tunnels cut into the walls at 50ft, coming out at 90ft. Barrel sponges and coral heads and fish teeming about make this an exhilarating experience.

North Pole Cave

Southwestern San Salvador.

This wall drops sharply from 40ft to more than 150ft. This site might as well have been called Santa's chimney, because there's a vertical cave that leads down to a crevice which in turn runs out over the wall at 110ft to 150ft.
There are more fish to be found at this reef than any other on this side of the island and once in a while a hammerhead shark may even swim by.

Hole in the Wall

Southwestern San Salvador.

King size crabs and granddaddy crawfish crawl the walls of deep crevices 50 to 110ft down. There's an amazing black coral tree at 90ft, and at every depth, scores of fish and rays swim by.

Long Island Regatta

The annual Long Island Sailing Regatta has been going for more than 30 years and is about the only time the island shakes off its sleepy vibe and comes out to party in style. Many of the younger generation who are off making their fortune return home for the four-day event (held in May or June) and islanders from all over the Bahamas come to compete. Open only to Bahamian sailboats, tourists are still more than welcome to come and join in with the eating, drinking and dancing.

WATERSPORTS

159

Diving with Grouper Fish, San Salvador

© The Bahamas Ministry of Tourism

Ship's Graveyard

Stella Maris, Long Island.

The 103ft-long steel freighter *MS Comberbach* sank in just 100ft of water off Long Island's coast. The beauty of this site is the wreck was prepped for optimal dive experience before it went down. There's an intact wheelhouse and the intact hull sits upright so you can swim right in and explore. The reef it sits near has multiple 50ft drop-offs.

Flamingo Tongue Reef

Stella Maris, Long Island.

Check out the ocean floor at this site and you'll understand the name. Thousands of colorful Flamingo Tongue cowrie shells litter the bottom. At only 25ft, it's a nice, easy dive.

Tartar Bank

Port Howe, Cat Island.

Five miles off shore lies a coral, sponge and sea fan-covered plateau. It slopes to a steep drop to about 6,000ft.

The Conqueror Wreck

Northeast of Long Island, off Rum Cay.

It hit a coral reef and sank in 1848, but it wasn't until 1969 that a group of divers from Hawaii's *Skin Diver Magazine* discovered the wreck of the *Conqueror*. The British Navy's first war vessel with a steam engine now sits in 25ft of water. Explore canons, canon balls, the shaft and engine.

Runway 10

Northwestern San Salvador.

If a plane failed to take off, chances are it would end up on this reef directly offshore in line with the international airport's runway. This particular sandy wall starts at 40 to 60ft, drops sharply to about 100ft and from there slopes gently down another 100ft or so. This wall is best done at night as that's when the basket starfish, octopus, crabs and pufferfish come out to play.

NIGHTLIFE

In a popular local song, the artist decides he's going to Cat Island to "join the rake 'n' scrape band." If you're looking for much more in the southern islands, you're in the wrong place. Most settlements have a local watering hole you can pop into for a cold drink and some good music.

Bridge Inn Bar

New Bight, Cat Island.
242-342-3013.

Friday and Saturday nights, this is the place to be. This is where you'll find Fealy & the Boneshakers, an honest to goodness rake 'n' scrape band. When they're taking a break, a jukebox fills in. The bar has all the basics covered.

Club Med

North of Riding Rock,
San Salvador. 242-331-2000.

Depending on resort occupancy, non-guests can usually score an evening pass for dinner, the bars and whatever entertainment the GOs have come up with for the night.

Driftwood Bar & Lounge

Riding Rock Inn, Cockburn Town,
San Salvador. 242-331-2631.

This rustic watering hole got its name for the pieces of driftwood patrons have collected, signed and left behind. The decor also features yacht T-shirts, business cards, and anything else scavenged from a stroll on the beach. Enjoy a drink at the bar or on the outdoor patio. Wednesday is disco night.

Stella Maris Resort

Stella Maris, Long Island.
242-338-2051/2/3.

The resort bar offers a variety of themed nights to keep the party going all week long. There's usually rake 'n' scrape here, too.

Stella Maris Resort Club

Clubroom at Stella Maris Resort

RESTAURANTS

The venues listed below were selected for their ambience, location and/or value for money. Rates indicate the average cost of an appetizer, entrée and dessert for one person (not including tax, gratuity or beverages). Most restaurants are open daily and accept major credit cards. Call for information regarding reservations, dress code and opening hours.

$$$$ Over $80   **$$** $20–$50
$$$ $50–$80   **$**   Under $20

INTRO

The Bahamas boasts a mouth-watering array of dining choices ranging from gourmet restaurants and trendy eateries to family-run diners, beach barbecues and lively fish fry gatherings. These casual affairs offer the best flavor of the Bahamas, not just in the delicious fresh fish they serve up, but also in the chance to mingle and party with the locals. The main islands of Nassau and Grand Bahama offer the widest choice of eating spots and this is where diners looking for a formal à la carte experience will be best served. The Out Islands offer a more rustic alternative with good local restaurants serving a variety of traditional Bahamian dishes.

Preparing conch salad at a conch stand, Nassau

© The Bahamas Ministry of Tourism

one of the region's top gourmet restaurants, while the megaresort of Atlantis on Paradise Island has added even more to the mix. On Grand Bahama Island, the huge resort of Our Lucaya and the lively Port Lucaya Marketplace are the places where the best restaurants can be found.

MID-RANGE

There's a wide choice across all the islands and on the Out Islands some of the best restaurants tend to be attached to hotels. These are the places to enjoy plenty of fresh fish and other Bahamian specialties.

LUXURY

Nassau carries the crown for eating out in style, having built up a reputation for fine dining with restaurants serving everything from Mexican and Creole to Chinese, Indian or Japanese cuisine. Graycliff in Nassau is known as

BUDGET

Some of the tastiest local fare can be sampled at the regular fish frys or beach barbecues and from roadside vendors who produce fabulous food at rock bottom prices.

NEW PROVIDENCE ISLAND

Graycliff

$$$$ **International**
8–12 West Hill Street, Nassau.
242 302 9150. www.graycliff.com.

This Georgian mansion and former pirate haunt and prison is one of the grandest hotels in the Bahamas and houses one of the Caribbean's top gourmet spots. Diners can take their pick from the world-renowned wine cellar containing a staggering 250,000 bottles and a selection of Graycliff's own hand-crafted cigars. The restaurant, said to be the only five-star eatery in the region, serves up a mix of international and Bahamian cuisine with an emphasis on seafood with dishes including Bahamian lobster tail, crab claws and trout. Opulent morsels include caviar, foie gras and truffles.

Shogun Revolver

$$$$ **Asian**
East Bay Street, Paradise Island
Bridge. 242 328 8383.
www.shogunrevolver.com.

For a taste of the Far East, come to this stylish eatery with its restaurant, lounge and terrace that have won plaudits from critics for the sophisticated ambience and good food. With its funky New York-style vibe and great views across the waterfront, the restaurant has carved out its own niche in the capital's restaurant scene. Diners can take their pick from modern Japanese dishes, including five- and seven-course tasting menus, and Shogun's selection of 20 different sakes.

©Ray Wadia/The Bahamas Ministry of Tourism

Wine cellar at Graycliff

Luciano's of Chicago

$$$ **Italian**
East Bay Street, Nassau.
242 323 7770/1. www.lucianos
nassau.com.

Enjoy *la dolce vita* amid the surroundings of a Tuscan-style sea-side villa, that houses this Italian restaurant. The elegant marble surroundings give a classy ambience to the waterfront location where diners can enjoy Italian dishes of seafood, pasta, steaks and antipasti along with notable Italian wines. Luciano's is regarded as one of the best value restaurants in the Bahamas with the high standards of service and food—and not so high prices. Enjoy the striking views across the harbor to Paradise Island where the skyline is dominated by the huge themed Atlantis complex.

Chez Willie

$$$ **French/Bahamian**
West Bay Street, Nassau (one block
west of the British Colonial Hilton
Hotel). 242 322 5364/6.
www.chezwillierestaurant.com.

Romantic elegance are the watchwords of this upscale gourmet spot, run by renowned Nassau restaurateur Willie Armstrong. It is famous for its slogan: "The only thing better than our food is our service." The food is more than memorable, with French Bahamian gourmet dishes that include mouth-watering temptations such as duckling breast in mango sauce or grilled lobster tail dipped in melted butter. The olde world ambience of this former prison makes it perfect for romantic dinners or leisurely dinner parties. Past guests have included former US president Richard Nixon and "ole blue eyes" himself, Frank Sinatra.

Cafe Matisse

$$$ Italian
Bank Lane (behind Parliament Square), Nassau. 242 356 7012. www.cafe-matisse.com.

Savor the arty ambience and soak up the history of this rustic eatery, located in the heart of downtown Nassau. Housed in a charming 18th century house, the restaurant's walls are lined with striking Matisse prints. Diners wanting to enjoy the balmy evenings can eat al fresco in the pretty courtyard or on the veranda. Homemade pasta, seafood and real Italian pizzas are the restaurant's specialties with temptations such as grilled lobster in cream sauce or roast duck with white porto and peaches.

The Poop Deck West

$$ American/Bahamian
West Bay Street, Sandyport, Nassau. 242 327 3325. www.the poopdeckrestaurants.com.

One of two restaurants (the other one is in the center of Nassau in East Bay Street) that are well known for their Bahamian seafood specialties, such as cracked conch and fried shrimp.

There's an extensive wine list, which helps to wash down some of the spicier dishes, and it's definitely worth trying the restaurant's special guava duff for dessert and its signature calypso coffee.

Goldies, Arawak Cay

$ Seafood
Arawak Cay, West Bay Street, Nassau (opposite Fort Charlotte).

Arawak Cay is one of the best places for authentic Bahamian seafood and is popular with locals as well as tourists who take the 30-minute walk or five-minute cab ride out of the city. There are numerous stands serving up tempting morsels—but Goldies is one of the best. Take your pick from lobster salad, steamed, grilled or fried fish, cracked conch and Goldie's famous Sky Juice—a heady mix of gin and coconut water.

Rita's Van

$ Bahamian
Woodes Rogers Walk, Nassau (by the Straw Market).

This is a favorite with the locals, so you know it must be good; and the simple, but tasty fare is a steal. It is popular with the lady vendors from the nearby Straw Market, and once you've tasted the food, you can see why. Fried fish and conch burgers are popular and one of Rita's specialties is chicken souse and rice (chicken wings and drumsticks cooked in stock with vegetables, onions and lime). It's marvelous.

Black Cod with Miso, Nobu, Atlantis

© Lee Pucker/Atlantis

PARADISE ISLAND

Nobu, Atlantis

$$$$ **Japanese**
Atlantis Paradise Island.
242 363 3000. www.atlantis.com.

Step into this stylish and buzzing enclave at the huge Atlantis resort to taste the latest creations inspired by famous chef Nobu Matisuhisa. The restaurant is next to the Atlantis casino and a Japanese pagoda surrounds the dining room. Visitors can take a seat at the sushi bar and chill out in the cocktail bar to the accompaniment of a mixture of Bahamian and Japanese musical diversions. Alternatively, diners can enjoy Nobu favorites such as new-style sashimi or the multi-course chef's choice Omasake. Bahamian favorites such as cracked conch and lobster have also been given the Nobu treatment and added to the menu.

Dune, Ocean Club, Paradise Island

$$$$ **French/Asian**
One&Only Ocean Club,
Paradise Island. 242 363 2501.
www.oneandonlyresorts.com.

The views alone make visiting this ultra-chic restaurant worthwhile. Built above the white sands of the beach, it has sweeping views over the ocean, and is definitely a place to see as well as be seen in. Award-winning chef Jean-Georges Vongerichten has brought the winning flair of his New York restaurants to the Bahamas, using lush local ingredients to create unforgettable French/Asian fusion cuisine. Open-air patios directly overlook the beach while the adjacent beachfront bar, which is open during the day, enjoys a fabulously romantic setting.

© 2007 One&Only

Dune, Ocean Club

Bobby Flay's Mesa Grill, The Cove, Atlantis

$$$$ **American/Bahamian**
The Cove, Atlantis Paradise Island.
242 363 6925. www.mesagrill.com.

Celebrated American chef Bobby Flay has brought his distinctive cuisine to the Bahamas. In fact he's brought it to The Cove, the upmarket all-suite property which

Bobby Flay's Mesa Grill

© Dana Neibert/Atlantis

is one of the newest additions to the sprawling Atlantis resort on Paradise Island. Mesa Grill is memorable in more ways than one, from the striking decor and fabulous views to the cuisine which combines Bobby's hallmark taste of America's southwestern states with the flavors of the Bahamas. The result is a delicious combination of dishes such as Bahamian spiced chicken skewers with yogurt cilantro sauce, shrimp and grouper ceviche or pineapple tequila sherbert with papaya meringues.

Bimini Road, Atlantis

$$$ Bahamian
Marina Village, Atlantis, Paradise Island. 242 363 3000. www. atlantis.com. See also p76.

If you're looking for live music and a lively atmosphere, this is a fun place to come. Located in the Marina Village at the Atlantis Resort on Paradise Island, Bimini Road is a colorful and vibrant hub where you can see Junkanoo bands performing. If you fancy something quieter, relax at the outdoor bar with one of the restaurant's signature mojitos. Inside, diners can see their dishes being prepared

in the impressive open kitchen, with its own conch station where fresh Bahamian conch is prepared to order. Diners can also take their pick from other tasty treats such as tamarind-glazed pork chops or mojo-marinated chicken and pineapple bread pudding, and the novel-sounding cookie-bash pie.

Columbus Tavern

$$ Bahamian
Paradise Island Drive, Paradise Island. 242 363 5923. www. columbustavernbahamas.com.

This claims to be Paradise Island's original waterfront restaurant and it makes a mean boast that it offers the freshest fish in Nassau! Diners can choose the seafood of their choice—be it lobster, crab, conch, mahi mahi or snapper and have it prepared to their own personal taste. Visitors can dine al fresco and couples feeling romantic can even have their meals served on a special floating dock—they just need to reserve it in advance.

GRAND BAHAMA ISLAND

China Beach

$$$ Asian
Our Lucaya Resort, Freeport. 242 373 1333. www.ourlucaya.com.

The focal point of this smart-casual restaurant is the show kitchen where you can see the chefs furiously chopping, boiling and frying away as they prepare the impressive selection of dishes reflecting the Pacific Rim. The attractive restaurant is set in its own building on the seafront at the huge Our

MUST EAT

China Beach at the Westin Grand Bahama Island Our Lucaya Resort

© Our Lucaya Resort

Lucaya resort, with views out to sea and across one of the resort's swimming pools.

La Dolce Vita

$$$ Italian
Port Lucaya Marketplace, Freeport. 242 373 8652.

This upmarket trattoria enjoys the reputation of being one of Freeport's finest Italian restaurants and promises the best espresso in town. Guests can take their pick from the choice of fresh pasta and Italian regional dishes—and even watch them being prepared by the chefs. Homemade ravioli with a variety of fillings, fresh mozzarella and carpaccio are some of the treats on the menu, while diners can choose to sit in the dining room or on the patio overlooking the marina.

Buccaneer Club

$$ Bahamian/Swiss
Deadman's Reef, Freeport. 242 349 3794.

The hillside setting makes this bistro a perfect place to catch

wonderful Bahamian sunsets over a dinner of delicious local specialties such as conch, grouper and crawfish. Shaped on a 19th century farmhouse with pretty terraces dotted with palm trees, the Buccaneer Club is more pub than restaurant with an informal ambience to match. The continental feel is helped by the foot-tapping alpine music, though local artworks dotting the walls reflect the West Indian theme.

Tony Macaroni

$$ Seafood
Taino Beach.

Catch the local rhythm at lively parties on Taino Beach where locals and visitors can feast on roasted conch cooked by local personality Tony Macaroni while dancing on the sands.
If you miss the Sunday afternoon Jazz on the Beach parties, you can catch the famous "Rake and Scrape on Da Beach" every Wednesday evening at 8pm or just simply turn up on other days to sample the local fare at Tony's beachside shack.

Bahamian specialties

Conch (pronounced konk) rules as the king of Bahamian cuisine. Many of the islands' specialties are based on seafood, but it is this large shellfish—more known for its beautiful shell—that you will find on most menus, either served raw, deep fried or steamed. It can also be added to added to salads or made into soups. Other delicacies include pea soup and dumplings, crab 'n' rice and grouper fingers. If this makes you thirsty, grab a can of the local Kalik beer or try a famous rum cocktail such as a Goombay Smash or Bahama Mama.

Bikini Bottom

$ **Bahamian/American**
Traveller's Rest, Williams Town Beach. 242 373 7951. www.bahamasvacationguide.com/bikinibottom.

A Bahamian beach hangout with good views, good company and good food. This is a popular haunt for tourists and locals who come to soak up the atmosphere and dance on the sands during the Saturday rake and scrape evenings with local band The Island Boys. The menu starts from just $2 and you can choose from tasty snacks such as cracked conch, Bikini Fettuccine, fried shrimp and American favorites such as hot dogs and burgers.

ANDROS AND BIMINI

Kamalame Cay Restaurant (Andros)

$$$$ **Caribbean**
Staniard Creek, Andros. 242 368 6281. www.kamalame.com.

Probably the best place to eat on the island with excellent food served up in the classy surroundings of The Great House. Set in the pretty resort of Kamalame Cay, the restaurant offers a delicious range of dishes combining the best local ingredients with international flavors. Local seafood is a specialty with lobster, shrimp or conch served up with tasty sauces. Lunchtimes are also a good time to visit, when succulent salads and rich pastas make an appearance. Reservations are required.

Kamalame Cay Restaurant

© The Bahamas Ministry of Tourism

MUST EAT

The Anchorage Restaurant & Bar (Bimini)

$$$ **American/Bahamian**
Kings Highway, Alice Town, Bimini. 242 347 3166.

Soak up the shades of Hemingway as the hell-raising author was a frequent visitor to the island. This restaurant is located at the Blue Water Resort, which contains Blue Marlin Cottage where Hemingway based his book, *Islands in the Stream*.

Those following in his footsteps today can stop off at the Anchorage to sample its tempting range of seafood dishes such as conch chowder and spiny broiled lobster or Bahamian fried chicken. The cooking is plain and simple and the end results are good. Alternatively, diners can admire the views of Alice Town Harbour through the picture windows.

Hank's Place (Andros)

$$ **Bahamian**
Fresh Creek, Andros. 242 368 2447. www.hanks-place.com.

This is Bahamian through and through. Owned and run by local Androsians (though up for sale), this local hangout is known for its tasty local fare. Located close to the bridge where the mail boats call, this is the place to come for Bahamian specialties such as conch fritters, grouper, wahoo, snapper along with seafood platters, steak and chicken. Then wash it down with the bar's bright pink signature cocktail, Hanky Panky! On warm evenings, meals are served in the Green Eyed Lady Bar built on its own deck over the

water—a handy place from which to feed leftovers to the fish.

Mangrove Cay Inn

$$ **Bahamian/American**
Mangrove Cay. 242 369 0069. www.mangrovecayinn.net.

This homely inn has a full service dining room where residents and visitors can tuck into Bahamian and American home-cooked meals, along with freshly baked breads and desserts. The wide-ranging menu includes seafood, chicken and pasta dishes along with steak platters and surf and turf combinations.

Petit Conch Restaurant (Bimini)

$$ **Bahamian/American**
South Bimini. 242 347 3500. www.biminisands.com

You'll find the Petite Conch tucked away on the second floor above the Bimini Sands Ship Store in South Bimini from where it opens for breakfast, lunch and dinner, serving a range of Bahamian and American cuisine. You can sit indoors or outside and choose from the menu's surf and turf choices with lobster or steak, or crab salads and other seafood delicacies, served up with fresh Bimini bread.

ABACOS ISLANDS

Mangoes

$$$ **International/Bahamian**
Marsh Harbour, Great Abaco. 242 367 2957.

Regarded as the best and most popular restaurant in the Abacos, Mangoes sits in one of Marsh

Harbour's most distinctive buildings and is popular with yachting types as well as locals. Seafood dishes are a popular option here and mangoes are liberally used across the menu to tasty effect. The restaurant is known for its conch burgers and fritters, but it's worth opting for the Taste of Abaco platter which contains these along with salad and shrimp, served on a wooden plank. This restaurant is good for lunches and dinners and Thursday and Sunday nights are spiced up by live music from a local rake 'n' scrape band. Reservations requested.

Wally's Restaurant

$$$ **Bahamian**
Bay Street, Marsh Harbour, Great Abaco. 242 367 2074

This is one of the most popular restaurants in the Bahamas and you can see why. With a promise that "nobody leaves here hungry" diners know they are in for a treat. Start off with Wally's Special cocktail—named after the owner Wally Smith—an intoxicating mix of fruit juices and rum, before choosing from the exotic menu that contains everything from dolphin burgers or conch cakes to Greek salad and New York steak. This distinctive pink colonial villa is a popular local haunt and the patio is the prime meeting spot, especially at lunchtimes.

Curly Tails Restaurant & Bar

$$ **Bahamian/Seafood**
Conch Inn, Marsh Harbour. Great Abaco. 242 367 4444. www.abacocurlytails.com.

Alistair and Harriet McDonald promise good old Bahamian hospitality at this picturesque restaurant, housed at the Conch Inn Hotel & Marina. Seafood is served up every way you can think of and is given a distinctive twist by the chef's use of Asian and Mediterranean ingredients along with sauces and soups containing tropical fruits and Caribbean vegetables. The fresh catch of the day is a good choice, while the best way to start or end the evening is with a cocktail on the restaurant's rooftop bar with its views over Marsh Harbour.

Nipper's Beach Bar & Grill, Great Guana Cay

$$ **Bahamian/Seafood**
Great Guana Cay. 242 365 5143. www.nippersbar.com.

If you're looking for somewhere that's lively and casual, then Nippers is for you. This popular spot attracts visitors and locals for its party atmosphere, good food and good swimming, snorkeling or diving as it overlooks the nearby Great Abaco Barrier Reef. If you don't fancy the beach, Nippers even has its own split-level swimming pool with a pool bar. There are two dining areas with great views across the ocean, and for lunch or dinner you can take your pick from lobster, chicken, grilled fish, burgers or salad. On Sundays

MUST EAT

Tippys restaurant

© Pineapple Fields

there is Nipper's famous Wild Boar Pig Roast, starting at 12.30pm, with its "all you can eat buffet" and occasional free concerts.

ELEUTHERA & HARBOUR ISLAND

Rock House Restaurant (Harbour Island)

$$$$ **International/Bahamian**
Rock House Hotel, Bay Street, Dunmore Town, Harbour Island. 242 333 2053. www.rockhouse bahamas.com.

A colonial-style culinary haven known for its exotic dishes and classy surroundings. The restaurant is part of the stylish Rock House hotel that has been transformed into an intimate and elegant retreat. Come here for the views over the bay and for food that combines Asian, Creole and Bahamian flavors. The restaurant is known for its jumbo Rock House crab cakes along with other temptations that include succulent salads and stone crabs accompanied with avocado and mango salad.

Tippy's Restaurant (Eleuthera)

$$$ **Bahamian**
Banks Road, Eleuthera. 242 332 3331. www.pineapplefields.com.

This hip beach bar offers casual, barefoot chic and is a magnet for islanders, visitors and the occasional celebrity. Located on a beautiful beach in the Pineapple Fields area between Governor's Harbour and Palmetto Point, Tippy's stands out as a collection of interlocking open-sided gazebos with a wraparound dining veranda. Diners enjoy not only the spectacular views, but also the delicious culinary creations (the fish and pasta are highly regarded) and live music on Friday and Sunday evenings in high season.

Sip Sip (Harbour Island)

$$ **International**
Court Street, Harbour Island. 242 333 3316.

This funky hangout is the place in Harbour Island to see and be seen. It's a chic spot for **lazy lunches**, especially as it closes at 4pm and doesn't open in the evenings. Its name comes from the Bahamian patois for gossip, no doubt fueled by regular customers such as supermodel, Elle McPherson, who owns a house on Harbour Island. Sip Sip has gained a reputation for serving mouth-watering lunches from an eclectic range of international cuisine, but also including tasty local dishes such as conch curry, coconut cakes and grilled shrimp.

Ma Ruby's Restaurant (Harbour Island)

$$ Bahamian
Tingum Village, Dunmore Town, Harbour Island. 242 333 2161. www.tingumvillage.com.

For a true Bahamian flavor, come to this restaurant and meet its famous owner Ma Ruby, whose homemade cooking has been made famous by singer Jimmy Buffett. This is the proud home of "Cheeseburgers in Paradise" as featured in Jimmy Buffett's *Parrot Head Handbook*. The restaurant's simple no-frills food and surroundings have won it a loyal audience. The restaurant can be found just off the main street, close to the beach, sitting snugly with a small

hotel and boutique. Taste Ma Ruby's seafood specials or one of her famous cheeseburgers, finished by her most popular dessert— Ma Ruby's Key Lime Pie.

Sammy's Place (Eleuthera)

$$ Bahamian
Albury's Lane, Rock Sound. 242 334 2121.

Sample a slice of local life at this local haunt, run by chef Sammy Culmer and his daughter Margeritta. Together, they serve up traditional Bahamian favorites such as conch fritters, peas 'n' rice, fried chicken and fish, and burgers. This is a place for good food, friendly service and low prices.

THE EXUMAS

Club Peace & Plenty Restaurant (Great Exuma)

$$$ International/Bahamian
Queen's Highway, George Town, Exuma. 242 336 2551. www.peaceandplenty.com.

The friendly house-party ambience of this well-known hotel extends to its restaurant with its relaxed air, good home-cooking and views over the sea.
The restaurant is regarded as one of the best on the island and is popular with the yachting crowd and passing celebrities. The cuisine is hail and hearty with dishes including conch burgers, tender steaks and seafood.
One of the restaurant's signature dishes is steamed grouper with sweet pepper, sautéed onions and tomatoes.

Club Peace and Plenty Restaurant

© "Club" Peace and Plenty Hotel

172

Cheater's Restaurant & Bar (Great Exuma)

$$ **Bahamian**
George Town. 242 336 2535.

Ask a taxi driver in Exuma where to eat and there's a good chance that he'll recommend this friendly and informal pad. Cheater's enjoys a good reputation on the island and is known for its freshly caught seafood, which is prepared to order. Conch chowder and conch fritters are among the specialties, though steak and chicken are also on the menu. Once you arrive, choose between sitting indoors or dining al fresco, where you can sit at the bar before your meal and admire the view over the ocean. Reservations are recommended.

Castaways (Great Exuma)

$$ **Bahamian**
Moss Town. 242 345 0248.

Situated just south of the airport, this casual restaurant is well known for its Bahamian culinary fare. Try the grouper fingers or fried snapper served up with the local staple peas 'n' rice, or tuck into delicious freshly cracked fried conch. If you fancy a truly Bahamian breakfast, this is the place to come for dishes such as stewed fish and grits.

LONG ISLAND

Anca's Away Restaurant & Bar

$$ **Bahamian**
Alligator Bay, Simms. 242 338 8593.

Stop at this local restaurant for breakfast, lunch or dinner where you can enjoy traditional Bahamian home-cooking. Choose from local favorite peas 'n' rice along with chicken dishes, ribs and seafood.

Max's Conch Bar & Grill

$ **Bahamian**
Deadman's Cay. 242 337 0056.

Don't drive past this quaint, rustic conch shack that sits by the side of the road in Deadman's Cay. Perch yourself on one of the handy bar stools, eat the good food and watch the world go by. If you want to taste a good conch salad, then this is the place to stop as it promises to serve the best one on the island. Other specialties guaranteed to set your tastebuds tingling include grilled conch, fish, soups and jerk chicken and pork.

SAN SALVADOR

New Columbus Tavern

$$ **Bahamian**
Victoria Hill. 242 331 2788.

In addition to the traditional Bahamian dishes of cracked conch, steamed and fried fish, barbecued spare ribs and lobster, this friendly hostellry also has a fine line in Italian-style pizzas. What's more, it will deliver them if you don't want to eat out. If you're feeling adventurous, try the Extravaganza Pizza which comes with virtually every topping you can think of, and wash it down with a famous Bahama Mama cocktail.

HOTELS

The properties listed below have been selected for their ambience, location and/or value for money. Prices reflect the average cost for a standard double room for two people (not including applicable taxes). Hotels in the Bahamas often offer special discount rates on weekends and off season. Quoted rates exclude the taxes for GST, PST and DMF which equal a total of 10%. See the earlier *Must See* sections for more information about the major resorts.

$$$$$	over $650	$$	$100–$250
$$$$	$400–$650	$	under $100
$$$	$250–$400		

INTRO

Visitors to the Bahamas will never be short of somewhere to stay: The islands offer a huge range of accommodation that takes in every type and style of lodging. This ranges from extravagant, glitzy resorts and big-name hotels to charming, family-run retreats and cozy guesthouses. Those wanting more independence can opt for the numerous villas and apartments which suit every taste and budget. The main islands of Nassau and Grand Bahama are home to the big resorts, but in the islands' quieter corners visitors can find tucked away fishing lodges and atmospheric hotels. The Out Islands have the monopoly on rustic retreats and the most luxurious of these have a firm following among the celebrity set.

LUXURY

The Bahamas does luxury very well with a good range of upmarket properties. First and foremost is the stunning One&Only Ocean Club on Paradise Island where the James Bond movie *Casino Royale* (2006) was shot. On the Out Islands, choose between the pretty Pink Sands hotel on Harbour Island or the impressive Abaco Club at Winding Bay.

MID-RANGE

There is a huge choice of properties in this category, ranging from all-inclusive resorts such as Super-Clubs® and Sandals® to international chains including Sheraton®, Westin®, Riu® and Wyndham®.

BUDGET

Travelers who are watching their pennies can choose between brands such as Best Western and Comfort Suites to smaller, locally run hotels and guest-houses. Not only do these add more of a local flavor to your stay, but they are good value too.

Coral Sands, Harbour Island

© Bahamas Tourist Office

NEW PROVIDENCE ISLAND

Graycliff Hotel & Restaurant

$$$$ **22 rooms**
8–12 West Hill Street, Nassau.
242 302 9150. www.graycliff.com.

This charming Georgian mansion dating from the 1750s is a romantic reminder of a bygone era. Nestled in the heart of Nassau, this former home of privateer John Howard Graysmith is an elegant reminder of Nassau's colonial years when it was established in 1844 as the city's first inn. Today, it boasts 20 beautifully and individually decorated bedrooms and suites.

🏖 Marley Resort & Spa

$$$$ **16 rooms**
West Bay Street, Cable Beach, Nassau. 242 702 2800. www.marleyresort.com.

Get a taste of the Marley legend at the reggae star's family holiday home that has been turned into a hotel and is run by his widow, Rita, and other members of his family. It prides itself on being a sanctuary of Caribbean and African style with hand-carved intricate touches throughout. Each of its themed rooms and suites is based on Marley song titles such as *Kinky Reggae*, *Talking Blues* and *Jammin'*. There's even a honeymoon suite that is appropriately called One Love.

Compass Point

© Compass Point

$$$ **20 rooms**
West Bay Street, Nassau. 242 327 4500. www.compasspointbeach resort.com.

This pretty boutique hotel with its brightly-painted cottages is chic and cheerful and a world away from some of Nassau's more extravagant resorts. Its location, just a ten-minute drive from Nassau's airport, makes it quick and easy

Bedroom at Marley Resort & Spa

© TMarley Resort & Spa

HOTELS

to get to. You also get some of the approaching planes flying overhead, though not too many to make this a problem. The hotel has its own small pool and sits above the small and pretty Love Beach, with a larger beach a few minutes' walk away.

Sandals Royal Bahamian Spa Resort & Offshore Island

$$$ **403 rooms**
Cable Beach, Nassau.
242 327 6400/2340.
www.sandals.com.

One of the flagship resorts of the Sandals® all-inclusive chain. This

Sandals Royal Bahamian Spa Resort & Offshore Island

palatial and ornate couples-only property sits on the white sands of Cable Beach overlooking its own private island, Sandals Cay. The island has two beaches and a swimming pool, while the main resort has seven pools, eight restaurants and 13 different categories of room, plus a Red Lane® Spa.

SuperClubs Breezes Nassau

$$$ **400 rooms**
Cable Beach, Nassau.
242 327 6153.
www.superclubs.com.

This Cable Beach all-inclusive resort is ideal for those wanting plenty to keep them occupied. Guests can fly on the trapeze in the circus school; bounce around in the trampoline clinics; or even try their hand at sumo wrestling, "bouncy boxing" and body painting before partying the night away at the hotel's Hurricanes Disco. Then there is a long list of watersports on offer along with the chance to go scuba diving or play golf at one of Nassau's courses nearby (for an extra charge). When it comes to eating and drinking, guests can choose from the resort's three bars and three restaurants.

Orange Hill Beach Inn

$$ **32 rooms**
Nassau. 242 327 5186.
www.orangehill.com.

This country-style inn boasts good views of the ocean thanks to its hilltop location and home-away-from-home ambience.
As well as its scenic location, it is also conveniently placed for the airport, which is just five minutes' drive away, and the center of Nassau, which is a short bus or taxi ride away. It has its own beach bar, restaurant and swimming pool and the rooms and apartments have their own kitchenettes.
The hotel also has a private cottage that can be rented out. Orange Hill offers special packages

© Bahamas Tourist Office

Villa at One&Only Ocean Club

© Barbara Kraft/One&Only Resorts

for families and divers and it is a popular stayover point for travelers on their way to or from one of the Out Islands.

PARADISE ISLAND

One&Only Ocean Club

$$$$$ **114 rooms**
Paradise Island Drive, Nassau. 242 363 2501. www.oneandonly oceanclub.com.

Arguably the Bahamas' most prestigious and expensive hotel, it oozes discreet sophistication and old-world glamor.
Set in 35 acres of lush grounds, this colonial hideaway provides an elegant escape from the frenetic atmosphere of Paradise Island. It's a perfect choice for budding James Bonds, as this was the setting for *Casino Royale*, and it revels in its beautiful surroundings. It even has its own 12th century Augustinian cloister that was shipped over from Lourdes and rebuilt. Then there's the superb Tom Weiskopf golf course, the Balinese-influenced Mandara spa, and the renowned Dune Restaurant by Jean-George Vongerichten.

The Cove, Atlantis

$$$$$ **600 suites**
Paradise Island, Nassau. 242 363 3000/2000. www.thecoveatlantis.com.

This is a classy retreat from the bustle of the main resort. Guests of The Cove can dip into Atlantis and its myriad attractions and retreat if it all becomes too much. The Cove has its own Cascades family pool area and sophisticated Cain at the Cove adult pool area, and these are reserved solely for The Cove guests. Dining options include the airy Mosaic buffet restaurant and Bobby Flay's Mesa Grill, which

Sapphire Suite Living Room, The Cove Atlantis

© Dana Neibert/Atlantis

HOTELS

177

boasts a great atmosphere and excellent food. The accommodation in this all-suite property is spacious and has the latest hi-tech accompaniments from plasma TVs to BOSE® entertainment systems.

Atlantis Paradise Island

$$$ 2,327 rooms
Paradise Island, Nassau. 242 363 3000. www.atlantis.com.

This megaresort is themed around the Lost City of Atlantis and prides itself on being bold, brash and totally unique. It is like a slice of Las Vegas in the Caribbean. The focal point is the huge waterscape, claimed to be the world's largest manmade open-air habitat with lagoons that are home to 50,000 sea creatures. There are thrilling water rides which are some of the most technically advanced in the world and The Dig, a maze of passageways built to resemble the ruins of the lost city of Atlantis. There are 11 swimming areas and more than 40 restaurants, lounges and bars plus a huge spa, fitness center and dolphin lagoon. Guests stay in the Beach Tower, which is the cheapest, followed by the Coral Towers and the striking and extravagant Royal Towers.

Paradise Island Harbour Resort

$$$ 247 rooms
Harbour Drive, Paradise Island, Nassau. 242 353 2561. www.paradiseislandbahama.com.

Set on the waterside, this all-inclusive complex is a short walk from the main beaches and attractions of Atlantis. But it has plenty of its own facilities too, including a large freeform pool with its own waterfall, two restaurants, a fitness center and a manmade "tanning beach." There is plenty for families, with a kids' club for youngsters and various children's facilities, plus numerous water sports and regular evening entertainment.

Comfort Suites

$$ 229 suites
1 Paradise Island Drive, Paradise Island, Nassau, 242 363 3680. www.comfortsuites.com.

Located just across the road from the Atlantis resort, Comfort Suites guests are able to use facilities at Atlantis, including the water attractions, spa and kids' club. They also have full privileges at Atlantis' restaurants and lounges. Comfort Suites has its own swimming pool and sits on a four-mile white-sand beach. The hotel restaurant serves breakfast and lunch.

Best Western Bay View Suites

$$ 30 units
Bay View Drive, Paradise Island, Nassau. 242 363 2555. www.bwbayviewsuites.com.

This is a peaceful haven, tucked away from the hubbub and excitement of Paradise Island. It is located on the southern hillside of the island, overlooking Nassau Harbour with villas, townhouses and one-bedroom suites spread through the lush grounds of palms and exotic plants. The resort has three swimming pools and a tennis court, and is ideally suited to couples, families and friends wanting a chance to experience the bright lights of Nassau without getting dazzled.

🧘 Sivananda Ashram Yoga Retreat

$ 53 rooms
Paradise Island, Nassau. 242 363 2902. www.sivananda bahamas.org.

The last place you'd expect to find a yoga retreat is among the glitzy extravagant hotels of Paradise Island, but this haven offers a breath of fresh air and a chance to revitalise body and soul. The property offers pleasant, simple rooms and cabins and there is also space for guests wanting to pitch their own tent. The emphasis of this retreat is on the yoga courses and sessions run by the teachers.

GRAND BAHAMA ISLAND

Old Bahama Bay

$$$ 79 rooms
West End. 242 350 6500. www.oldbahamabay.com.

This atmospheric hotel, designed in typical Bahamian and colonial style, is located at West End—the island's closest point to Florida 56 miles away. It was originally owned by British holiday camp pioneer Billy Butlin, who designed it as the first upmarket all-inclusive island resort, boasting its own airfield and the largest swimming pool in the Western Hemisphere. Having gone into decline it reopened in 2001 as Old Bahama Bay and still boasts the huge pool, measuring 4,000 sq ft, plus a marina, sports

facilities and the most extensive snorkel trail program in the region.

Our Lucaya Resort

$$ 1,230 rooms
Seahorse Road, Royal Palm Way, Freeport. 242 373 1333 or 242 373 1444. www.ourlucaya.com.

© Our Lucaya Resort
Sheraton Grand Bahama Island Our Lucaya

This megaresort comprises two hotels, the Westin Our Lucaya and the Sheraton Our Lucaya, and combines modern facilities with traditional Bahamian touches. The complex is one of the biggest in the Bahamas and boasts two excellent golf courses, The Reef and The Lucayan, the Butch Harmon School of Golf, a huge spa and fitness center plus a casino. It sits in 372 acres, fronted by a 7.5-acre white-sand beach and contains 14 restaurants and cafes.
There's plenty to amuse children, too, with a kids' activity center and Camp Lucaya children's club. Our Lucaya has been named as one of the best Caribbean family resorts.

Pelican Bay at Lucaya

© Pelican Bay at Lucaya

Pelican Bay at Lucaya

$$ 183 rooms
*Seahorse Road, Freeport. 242 373
9550. www.pelicanbayhotel.com.*

This small luxury hotel combines
the romance of the Caribbean
with sophisticated European
design and Danish influence. It is
also in an ideal location overlook-
ing Port Lucaya Marina. This makes
it convenient for guests wanting
to be close to the action of Port
Lucaya Marketplace with its shops,
bars, restaurants and live bands,
without being part of it. The hotel
prides itself on its romantic laid-
back ambience, complemented by
its newly-opened waterfront Sabor
Restaurant and Bar.

Viva Wyndham
Fortuna Beach

$$ 276 rooms
*Churchill Drive & Fortuna Road,
Freeport. 242 373 4000. www.viva
wyndhamresorts.com.*

Sporty, fun-loving types will love
this 276-room resort which has
its own 1,200ft white sand beach.
With three restaurants, bars, a
disco, and a host of activities
including diving, fishing and
sunset cruises, there is plenty to
do. In addition there's a kids' club

and a new Viva Circus offering
thrilling acrobatic performances,
stunts and trapeze lessons. And
as the resort is all-inclusive, it is all
included in the price.

ANDROS, BERRY
AND BIMINI ISLANDS

Small Hope Bay Lodge
(Andros)

$$$ 21 rooms
*Fresh Creek. 242 368 2013.
www.smallhope.com.*

The first thing that strikes you at
this resort is the silence—bar the
gentle lapping of the waves on the
beautiful golden sands and the
occasional call of seabirds. This is a
simple island getaway which offers
a true escape—and it has been
welcoming visitors since 1960,
making it one of the Bahamas'
most established hotels. Compris-
ing wooden cottages, scattered
along the beachfront, with brightly
decorated furnishing, Small Hope
Bay was the first diving resort in
the Bahamas and it is still run by
the same family. Not surprisingly,
divers make up most of the guests
but the resort also appeals to
couples or families looking for
a relaxing holiday with just the
beach and the sea for company.

Small Hope Bay Lodge

© The Bahamas Ministry of Tourism

The resort is all-inclusive and at mealtimes everyone eats together, the staff and the family too. Children are catered for with their own playroom and free babysitting in the early evening.

Bimini Big Game Resort & Marina (Bimini)

$$ **47 rooms**
King's Highway, Alice Town. 242 347 3391. www.biminibig game.com.

Bimini Big Game Resort & Marina

© The Bahamas Ministry of Tourism

This renowned resort is known as the center of marine sports in the Bahamas, attracting loyal guests back year after year. It is popular for its club-like atmosphere and offshore waters that have made this area one of the world's best for fishing, diving and boating. The resort boasts its own marina, restaurant, bar and an extensive line-up of sporting facilities.

Emerald Palms (Andros)

$$ **50 rooms**
Driggs Hill, South Andros. 242 369 2713. www.emerald-palms.com.

This intimate hideaway is tucked away on some of the most secluded and romantic beaches in the Bahamas. The cottages and villas are spread over 10 acres of

coconut palm groves leading to the powder white sands. Guests have the choice of biking, kayaking, bird-watching, fishing and nature tours. The hotel has its own restaurant and swimming pool and is planning to open a children's activity center.

Sea Crest Hotel and Marina (Bimini)

$$ **25 rooms**
Alice Town, North Bimini. 242 347 3495.

You will find this unassuming hotel in the center of Alice Town, not far from the beach. It has its own marina and a restaurant for breakfast and lunch; there are plenty of options nearby for dinner.
All rooms have ocean or bay views, cable TV, small refrigerators and air conditioning. Two- and three-bedroom suites are also available.

ABACOS ISLANDS

Abaco Club at Winding Bay

$$$$$ **70 rooms**
Marsh Harbour, Abaco. 242 367 0077. www.theabacoclub.com.

This luxurious castaway-style retreat is the brainchild of British entrepreneur Peter de Savary and run by the upmarket Ritz-Carlton® hotel group. Set over a staggering 534 acres, it has a fabulous Scottish-style tropical links golf course (the first of its type in the world) along with a host of first-class sporting facilities and a spa. The resort has been set up as a private members' club, but temporary guests are welcome.

Abaco Beach Resort

$$ **92 rooms**
Marsh Harbour, Abaco. 242 367 2158. www.abacoresort.com.

This resort is regarded as the biggest and the best in Marsh Harbour. Set in 52 acres of lush gardens on the waterfront where it has its own 190-slip marina and watersports center, the hotel also has two tennis courts and bikes for hire so guests can explore the island. Its Angler's Restaurant is one of the best in the locality.

Bluff House

$$ **36 rooms**
Green Turtle Cay, Abaco. 242 365 4247. www.bluffhouse.com.

This former private home still exudes the same cozy ambience that makes you feel more like a friend than a guest. Set on the highest bluff on Green Turtle Cay, it has 36 rooms, suites, villas and cottages, a beautiful private beach, its own marina, two restaurants, two bars, a new tennis court and a swimming pool. There is also entertainment twice a week. All rooms have views across the ocean, air conditioning and a daily maid service. Children under 12 stay for free.

Abaco Beach Resort

© Bahamas Tourist Office

Green Turtle Club & Marina

© The Bahamas Ministry of Tourism

Green Turtle Club & Marina

$$ **31 rooms**
PO Box AB-22792, Green Turtle Cay, Abaco. 242 365 4271. www.greenturtleclub.com.

A Tipsy Turtle Rum Punch greets guests at this laidback resort where its rooms are said to re-semble "England in the tropics." It is regarded as one of the premier resorts of the Out Islands and has been listed in *The 100 Best Resorts of the Caribbean*. It is famous for its relaxed ambience and excellent restaurant and also has a 40-slip marina.

Abaco Inn

$ **22 rooms**
Elbow Cay, Abaco. 242 366 0133. www.abacoinn.com.

This cozy property, nestled among coconut palms on a ridge of daz-zling white sand dunes, prides it-self on offering barefoot elegance. Its 12 recently refurbished cottage rooms, eight one-bedroom villas and one two-bedroom suite overlook the Atlantic Ocean and tranquil Abaco Sound. Guests can spend their time fishing, diving, snorkeling or simply relaxing on the beach or around the pool.

MUST STAY

ELEUTHERA & HARBOUR ISLAND

Pink Sands
(Harbour Island)

$$$$$ **25 rooms**

PO Box 87, Chapel Street, Harbour Island, Eleuthera. 242 333 2030. www.pinksandsresort.com.

An upmarket celebrity hideout, owned by Island Records founder Chris Blackwell, which has attracted the likes of movie star Julia Roberts and is one most sought-after places to stay. The one- and two-bedroom cottages are exquisitely decorated with local artwork and batik fabrics. Some have their own private pathways to the beach and expansive wooden decks complete with hot tubs overlooking the ocean. Eating here is a treat with four-course dinners served up on the candlelit terrace of the Garden Terrace restaurant.

Pink Sands

© The Bahamas Ministry of Tourism

Coral Sands
(Harbour Island)

$$$ **36 rooms**

PO Box 54, Chapel Street, Harbour Island, ELeuthera. 242 333 2350. www.coralsands.com.

A place for lovers, particularly beach lovers, as this hotel sits on a fabulous three-mile, pink-sand beach. There are 39 rooms, newly restored in British colonial style, full of warm woods and crisp linens. Guest can chill out on the beach, by the pool or rent a boat and go snorkeling and diving.

The Landing
(Harbour Island)

$$$ **7 rooms**

PO Box 190, Harbour Island, Eleuthera. 242 333 2707. www.harbourislandlanding.com.

A gracious colonial mansion that overlooks the harbor in Dunmore Town and enjoys a reputation as one of the hippest addresses on Harbour Island. Just a few minutes from the beach, its rooms have been designed by aristocratic designer India Hicks in classic plantation style with colonial influences. The hotel is only a few minutes' walk from Harbour Island's famous pink sand beach, though The Landing also has its own sheltered swimming pool and a good restaurant that is the hub of the local social scene.

Romora Bay
(Harbour Island)

$$$ **22 rooms**

PO Box ELH-27146, Harbour Island, Eleuthera. 242 333 2325. www.romorabay.com.

This hotel boasts the best sunsets you will find anywhere—an ideal setting for couples wanting to marry on the pink-sand beach nearby. There are 22 boutique-style rooms spread across four acres along with two restaurants, two bars, tennis court and an infinity-edge pool.

HOTELS

Rock House (Harbour Island)

$$$ **9 rooms**

Bay Street, PO Box EL-27239, Harbour Island. 242 333 2053. www.rockhousebahamas.com.

Guests have been coming to this Harbour Island bolthole since the 1940s. It has now evolved into a hotel with ten bedrooms, known by whimsical names such as Parrot, Pineapple or Seahorse. In addition to the main dining room, there is a poolside martini bar which has a big screen TV. The hotel also has its own private section of beach where guests can take picnic baskets.

Quality Inn Cigatoo (Eleuthera)

$$ **22 rooms**

Haynes Avenue, PO Box EL86 Governor's Harbour, Eleuthera. 242 332 3060. www.qualityinn.com.

This pretty hotel, surrounded by palm trees on a hillside overlooking Governor's Harbour, is part of the Choice Hotels® group. Its quiet location makes it an ideal hideaway for couples who can enjoy the swimming pool, tennis court, and attractive gardens. There is also an Italian restaurant, complete with an extensive wine cellar. The resort is not recommended for children under 16.

THE EXUMAS

Four Seasons Resort Great Exuma at Emerald Bay

$$$ **180 rooms**

Queens Highway, Great Exuma. 242 336 6800. www.fourseasons. com/greatexuma.

Four Seasons Resort Great Exuma at Emerald Bay

© The Bahamas Ministry of Tourism

For couples looking for unadulterated luxury in an exclusive Bahamian setting, the Four Seasons® hotel has everything you could hope for. It is one of the largest resorts in the Out Islands, with 174 rooms, six one-bedroom suites, one villa, and 18 private residences, an 18-hole Greg Norman golf course, spa and health club, and two swimming pools.

Palm Bay Beach Club (Great Exuma)

$$$ **70 rooms**

George Town, Great Exuma. 242 336 2787. www.palmbaybeach club.com.

This tranquil cottage resort offers true escapism in beautiful surroundings on the white sands of Elizabeth Harbour. With two swimming pools, hot tubs, a

MUST STAY

beach bar and grill, plus numerous watersports, guests can do as little or as much as they want.

Peace & Plenty (Great Exuma)

$$ 32 rooms
George Town, Exuma. 242 336 2551. www.peaceandplenty.com.

You can choose between the original Club Peace and Plenty, which is the hub of the action in this part of Great Exuma, or the newer 16-room Beach Inn nearby. The Club is the livelier of the two, with evening entertainment, which includes live calypso, karaoke and an Elvis impersonator. The hotel is close to the beach and also runs its own ferry to the beach on nearby Stocking Island.
All rooms have air conditioning, a mini-fridge and satellite TV.

CAT ISLAND

Fernandez Bay Village

$$ 18 rooms
New Bight, Cat Island. 242 342 3043. www. fernandez bayvillage.com.

This remote, rustic, family-owned resort, which opened in 1980, prides itself on its house party atmosphere. There are 15 villas, strung along the beach; the beach bar runs on an honor system, and shoes are optional. Guests can spend their days fishing, boating, snorkeling or lazing in a hammock and in the evening, candlelit dinners are held around a beach bonfire.

Hawk's Nest Resort & Marina

$$ 12 rooms
New Bight, Cat Island. 242 342 7050. www.hawks-nest.com.

Set on the southern tip of Cat Island, this resort describes itself as a "tropical paradise" with its dive center, private airstrip, pub and marina. There are ten colorful ocean-front rooms and Point House—a two-bedroom beach villa, perfect for couples, families or groups of friends.

Sammy T's Beach Resort

$$ 8 rooms
Bennett's Harbour, Cat Island. 242 354 6009. www.sammyt bahamas.com.

If you want to spend your days lazing on a deserted pink-sand beach and your nights in a uniquely decorated wooden villa, then come here. Run by local Sammy Thurston (aka Sammy T), this intimate resort offers watersports from its own private beach and meals at its Sapodilla Restaurant.

LONG ISLAND

⚓ Cape Santa Maria Beach Resort

$$$ 44 rooms
Galliot Cay, Seymours. 242 338 5273. www.capesantamaria.com.

Set on the stunning sweep of one of the most beautiful beaches in The Bahamas, this stylish hotel promises barefoot elegance. Its 20 bungalows open directly onto the gently-curving bay, each with private verandas from where to watch beautiful sunsets.

BAHAMAS

A

Abaco National Park 124
Abacos 116
    Boating and Sailing 126
    Bonefishing 126
    Deep Sea Fishing 127
    Diving 127
    Getting Around 117
    Historic Buildings 121
    Hotels 117, 181
    Kayaking 127
    Museums and Galleries 123
    Parks and Gardens 124
    Resorts 117
    Restaurants 169
    Watersports 126
Wild Dolphin Encounters 127
Accessibility 21
Accommodation 21
Acklins Island 146
Adelaide Beach 38
Adelaide Village 47, 51
Albert Lowe Museum 123
Alice Town Trio 107
Allan's Cay 142
Amberjack Reef 144
America's Cup Sailing 58
Andros 100
Andros, Berry and Bimini 100
    Beaches 107
    Big Game Fishing 114
    Bonefishing 114
    Dive Operators 113
    Dive Sites 112
    Historic Sites 111
    Hotels 102, 180
    Museums 108
    Natural Sites 110
    Parks and Gardens 109
    Resorts 102
    Restaurants 168
    Spas 106
    Watersports 112
Andros Barrier Reef 112
Androsia Batik Factory 111
Aquaventure at Atlantis 74
Arawak Cay 47
Ardastra Gardens 52

B

Bahamas Historical Society 43
Bahamas National Trust 46
Bahamian Heritage Centre 43
Balcony House 40
Bat cave in Hatchet Bay 135
Bathing Beach, Shell Beach &
    French Wells 152
Bay Street 54
Ben's Cavern 94
Berry Islands, The 101
Bimini Islands, The 101
Bimini Museum 108
Bimini Road 113
Bird Rock Lighthouse 155
Blue Hole 110
Botanic Gardens 45
Business Hours 22
Butler, Sir Milo 42

C

Cabbage Beach 70
Cable Beach 38
Cable Beach Golf Course 56
Calendar of Events 12
Cape Santa Maria Beach 152
Cartwright's Cave 158
Cat Island 146
Caves, The 46
Cenotaph 40
Central Andros National Park 109

Chamberlain Kendrick House 121
Chicago Herald Monument 158
Christ Church Cathedral 39
Cigars 55
Cloisters 71
Club Med Beach 132
Coco Plum Beach 141
Columbus, Christopher 26, 30
Columbus Cove 158
Columbus Landing Cross 158
Communications 22
Conch Sound Blue Hole 112
Coral Beach 84
Crooked Island 146
Crystal Court 72
Current Cut 136
Customs 18

D

Deal's Beach 153
Dean's Blue Hole 157, 159
Devil's Backbone 136
Disabled Travelers 21
Discount Booking Websites 22
Dixon Hill Lighthouse 155
Dolphin Cay 75
Dolphin Encounters 52
Dolphin Experience, The 96
Doolittle's Grotto 159
Drug Laws 17
Dunmore Town 128

E

Earth & Fire 72
East Beach 153
Electricity 22
Eleuthera 128
**Eleuthera and
Harbour Island 128**
    Beaches 132
    Dive Sites 136
    Hotels 129, 182
    Natural sites 134
    Nightlife 137

    Resorts 129
    Restaurants 171
    Surf School 137
    Watersports 136
Eleutheran Adventurers 27
Exuma Cays, The 138
Exuma Cays Land and
    Sea Park, The 142
Exumas, The 138
    Beaches 140
    Boat Rentals 145
    Dive Sites 144
    Golf 144
    Hotels 139, 184
    Kayaking 145
    Natural Sites 142
    Outdoor Sports 144
    Resorts 139
    Restaurants 172
    Swim with Dolphins or Pigs 145
    Tennis 144
    Watersports 144

F

Family Islands 27
Fantasia Tours 97
Farquharson Plantation 154
Flamingo Tongue Reef 160
Fort Charlotte 39
Fort Fincastle 40
Fort Montagu 41
Fortune Beach 84
Fortune Hills Golf and
    Country Club 93
Fountain Bay Beach 153
Fountain of Youth 110
Freeport 79
French Bay 153

G

Gallop on the Beach 53
Gambier Village 51
Garden of the Groves 87
George Town 138

INDEX

Getting Around 19
Getting There 18
Glass Window, The 134
Gold Rock (Ben's) Blue Hole 95
Gold Rock Beach 85
Gold Rock Creek 88
Government House 41
Grand Bahama 78
   Beaches 84
   Casinos 83
   Dive Sites 94
   Golf 93
   Historic Sites 89
   Horseback Riding 94
   Hotels 80, 179
   Natural Sites 88
   Nature Tours 92
   Nightlife 98
   Outdoor Sports 93
   Parks and Gardens 86
   Resorts 80
   Restaurants 166
   Shopping 90
   Snorkeling 97
   Tennis 93
   Watersports 94
Grand Bahama Nature Tours 92, 97
Great Abaco 116
Great Exuma 138
Great Guana Cay 116
Great Inagua Lighthouse 155
Green Cay Bird Colony 109
Green Turtle Cay 116
Green Turtle Cay Cemetery 121
Gregory Arch 48

H

Haines Cay Beach 108
Hamilton's Cave 157
Happy Trails 57
Harbour Island 128
Harrold and Wilson Ponds
   National Park 45
Havana Trading Company 91

Health 18
Hemingway, Ernest 108
Heritage Trail, The 89, 92
Hermitage, The 89
History 26
Hole in the Wall 159
Hope Great House 156
Hope Town 116
Hope Town Lighthouse 121
Hotels 174

I

Inagua 146
Inagua National Park 156
International Bazaar 91
International Cultural Festival 45
International Visitors 17

J

Jacaranda House 41
James Point Beach 133
Johnston's Foundry & Gallery 123
Jose, The 95
Junkanoo 31

K

Know Before you Go 16

L

Lake Victoria 143
Lighthouse, The 71
Little Exuma 138
Long Island 147
Lost City of Atlantis 110
Love Beach 152
Lucaya 79
Lucayan Beach 85
Lucayan Golf Course 93
Lucayan National Park 86
Lucayans, The 30

INDEX

M

Mailboats 21, 135
Mamma Rhoda Rock 113
Man O'War 116
Marina Village 72
Marsh Harbour 116
Media 23
Memorial Sculpture Garden 125
Money 23
Moray Alley 113
Mount Alvernia 157
Mount Alvernia Hermitage 154
Mysterious Cave 144

N

Nassau 30
Nassau Public Library 41
National Art Gallery of the
  Bahamas 43
Neem tree 125
New Providence 30
  Beaches 38
  Casinos 37
  Diving 59
  Driving Tour 50
  Fishing 58
  For Kids 52
  Golf 56
  Historic Buildings 39
  Historic Sites 46
  Horseback Riding 57
  Hotels 32, 175
  Kiteboarding 60
  Museums and Galleries 43
  Natural Sites 46
  Nightlife 62
  Outdoor Sports 56
  Parks and Gardens 45
  Resorts 32
  Restaurants 163
  Shopping 54
  Snorkeling 60
  Spas 36
  Walking Tour 48
  Watersports 58

New World Museum 154
Nightlife 62, 76, 98, 137, 161
  Aura 76
  Bahama Mama Sunset Cruise
    and Show 98
  Bambu 62
  Bimini Road Restaurant 76
  Bridge Inn Bar 161
  Cain at the Cove 77
  Club Amnesia 98
  Club Med 161
  Club Waterloo 62
  Count Basie Square 99
  Driftwood Bar & Lounge 161
  Flamingo 62
  Fluid Lounge & Nightclub 62
  Green Parrot Bar & Grill 63
  Gusty's 137
  Joker's Wild Comedy Club 77
  Junkanoo at Marina Village 77
  Native Slice at Club Amnesia 99
  Prop Club Sports Bar &
    Dance Club, The 99
  Seagrapes 137
  Senor Frogs 63
  Shenanigans 99
  Stella Maris Resort 161
  Vic-Hum 137
Norman's Cay 143
North Pole Cave 159

O

Ocean Club Golf Course 73
Ocean Hole Rock Sound 134
Old Gaol, The 122
Out Islands 27
Over The Hill 31

P

Papa Doc's Wreck 95
Paradise Beach 70
Paradise Island 64
  Beaches 70
  Casinos 69
  Golf 73

Historic Buildings and
  Gardens 71
Hotels 65, 177
Nightlife 76
Outdoor Sports 73
Resorts 65
Restaurants 165
Shopping 72
Spas 68
Tennis 73
Watersports 74
People to People 47
Peterson's Cay National Park 95
Pink Flamingos 156
Pink Sands Beach 132
Pirates of Nassau 53
Pleasant Bay 38, 51
Pompey Museum of Slavery
  and Emancipation 44
PopPop Studios 44
Port Lucaya 90
Power Boat Adventures 75
Practical Information 16
Preacher's Cave in Eleuthera 135
Public Buildings, Nassau 42
Public holidays 23

Q

Queen's Staircase, The 46

R

Rand Nature Center 86
Reef Course 93
Regatta, George Town 145
Regatta, Long Island 159
Rental Houses, Abacos 120
Resorts 32, 65, 80, 102, 117, 129,
  139, 148, 174
Restaurants 24, 162
Retreat Gardens, The 46
Rogers, Woodes 27, 30
Rolle Town 143
Rolleville 143
Runway 10 160

S

Saddle Cay Beach 140
Sandy Point 153
San Salvador 147
Saunders Beach 38
Sea Star II Wreck 95
Segway Tours 57
Shark Alley 95
Shark Reef 159
Ship's Graveyard 160
Smiling Pat's Adventures 88
Smith's Point Fish Fry 89
Smoking 25
Southern Island Lighthouses 155
South Islands 146
  Beaches 152
  Dive Sites 159
  Historic Buildings and
    Museums 154
  Historic Sites 158
  Hotels 148, 185
  Natural Sites 157
  Nightlife 161
  Parks and Gardens 156
  Resorts 148
  Restaurants 173
  Watersports 159
Souvenirs 55
Spanish Wells 128
Spectator Sports 25
SPID City 95
Sponging and Weaving Straw 111
Sports 25, 57
St Andrew's Presbyterian
  Church 42
Stargate Blue Hole 113
Stocking Island 141
Straw Market 55
Sugar Beach 108
Summer Set Beach 107
Sun & Sea Outfitters 91
Surfer's Beach 133
Surrey Ride 54

INDEX